Organized Enough

Organized Enough

The Anti-Perfectionist's Guide to Getting—and Staying—Organized

———

Amanda Sullivan

Da Capo
LIFE
LONG

Copyright © 2017 by Helen Amanda Sullivan

Designed by Trish Wilkinson
Set in 11.5-point Adobe Caslon Pro by Perseus Books

Cataloging-in-Publication data for this book is available from the Library of Congress.

First Da Capo Press edition 2017
ISBN: 978-0-7382-1932-5 (paperback)
ISBN: 978-0-7382-1933-2 (e-book)

Published by Da Capo Press, an imprint of Perseus Books, LLC, a subsidiary of Hachette Book Group, Inc.
www.dacapopress.com

Da Capo Press books are available at special discounts for bulk purchases in the U.S. by corporations, institutions, and other organizations. For more information, please contact the Special Markets Department at Perseus Books, 2300 Chestnut Street, Suite 200, Philadelphia, PA 19103, or call (800) 810-4145, ext. 5000, or e-mail special.markets@perseusbooks.com.

10 9 8 7 6 5 4 3 2 1

For my clients, who made me an organizer

CONTENTS

INTRODUCTION

> There are some enterprises in which a careful
> disorderliness is the true method.
> —HERMAN MELVILLE, *MOBY DICK*

Coco was ready to change. A striking woman, Coco is an actor, playwright, and film editor. After years of being a "starving artist," she was now actually making money, but she wasn't really feeling in control. Her tiny New York apartment in Hell's Kitchen was becoming cave-like as her clutter grew, overflowing from bookshelves, burying surfaces, and piling up in corners. From digital equipment to folders of financial records, an ongoing film project was claiming precious floor space. Coco also still had items from her former career as a musician that she no longer used but didn't quite know what to do with. Everything demanded her attention, but she was busy. Just thinking about dealing with all the paper piles made her anxious. To top it all off, her deep commitment to the environment made it hard for her to just throw things away.

Coco wasn't alone. A little farther uptown, Jana was busy squirreling away tote bags—full of magazines to read, gifts to give, clothes she shouldn't have bought, and hand-me-downs she didn't really need from friends who were organizing their closets. She filled the bags up and tucked them away. Now her own closets had become unusable.

Still farther north, in Riverdale, Ginny and Evan were drowning in kid stuff: knapsacks, gifts from Grandma, scooters, and art supplies. They tried to get organized, and they bought plastic bins and boxes to house it all, but no matter what they did, the clutter always seemed to grow back.

Sound familiar? In all of these cases, the solution wasn't just "straightening up." Over the years, one thing I've realized is that whether a home looks like a junk shop or whether it's so pristine that I initially wonder why I've been summoned, there is usually some layer of perfectionism or unrealistic expectations getting in the way of the real, necessary, and practical changes that can and should be made.

When I work with people, I want to dig deep and help them figure out how their piles and cluttery situations evolved. What is the point if I make it better only to have it revert after I go? I want you to be easily able to maintain order once it is restored.

The Limits of Perfection

"Your book is the anti-perfectionist's guide to organizing? But your business is called The Perfect Daughter!" a client exclaimed when I told her I was writing this book.

Indeed. In a way, my entire life has been an exploration of the concept of perfection and control. When I was growing up, it felt like no matter how hard I tried, it was never good enough for my mother. I love my mother, and I am so grateful now for all that she taught me, but she had high standards. When I would tell people that she once pulled me out of one school and put me into a more rigorous one because my grades were too *high*, they would laugh, but it was true!

Still, she had drilled in me attention to detail. When I first started my organizing business, it was with my mother's housekeeping standards in mind and the idea that I could help clients do all the things a "perfect daughter" would help you do, if she wasn't busy living in another state, running a company, or raising a family. Time has moved on, though. Now that I am a mother (my daughter likes to say that *she* is the perfect daughter), if my three children have taught me anything, it is that I am *not* perfect. Moreover, I've realized that the quest for perfection is the root of the problem, not its solution.

In my sixteen years as a professional organizer, I have learned that people may want perfection when it comes to their homes, but they do not *need* perfection. In truth, getting hung up on being perfectly organized actually gets in the way. People don't need a color-coded labeling system or a kitchen so neat it looks like it came out of a design magazine. They don't need to downsize to eighty-four square feet of living space to reduce clutter. These are not sustainable practices, and when we can't attain them, we feel like failures and give up. Instead, people need to make organization invisible, so that their lives run more smoothly and so that they have a feeling of control and peace. They need to be *organized enough*.

I have helped hundreds of clients—from hoarders to celebrities to ordinary families—become organized enough. The goal is always ease and functionality over photo-readiness. In this book, I'll provide you with alternative ways of thinking

xii   *Introduction*

about your home, your stuff, and your clutter. Adjusting your perspective is often the most powerful tool for creating lasting change, but few people know how to look—and I mean *really look*—at their homes. On one hand, disorder and disarray should not reign. The easy accessibility of cheap stuff threatens to overwhelm everyone's living space. But, on the other, should a home look like a still life from *Elle Decor*? Not really. It would be hard for it to function day in and day out. The pages of Pinterest and many of the shows on HGTV fill us with unrealistic expectations of what a home should be. Change is needed, but it isn't about looking like a picture in a magazine. It is about taking control of your life so you don't fritter it away managing your possessions.

The most wonderful homes are those that are both alive and serene. When you come home, you should feel a sense of peace and order, not stress and anxiety.

When I wake up in the morning, before the rest of my family gets up, I take a few minutes to sit on my seventeen-year-old couch, drink some coffee, and contemplate my bookcase. I have a lot of books—I'm not a minimalist. My books are not alphabetized or arranged by color (which I find an appalling trend), but in general sections: travel, biography, classics, mysteries, Shakespeare. (The self-help I keep in the bedroom.) I like to look at the books as I let my mind wander. It's a very peaceful start to the day.

Then, I make breakfast. I go into my kitchen, where the countertops are clean and free of dirty dishes, but not perfectly cleared off. For example, I keep a little pot of sea salt and a bottle of olive oil on the counter. I could fit them in the cabinet, but why? I reach for them several times a day, and to me they make my kitchen look like a place where cooking happens, which it is. Every room in my house has something like that—items and collections that some organizers might tell you "shouldn't" be there but to me make it home. More specifically, *my* home. What special objects make yours?

This is not a book that will tell you to throw everything out and live in a white box. How boring! I want your house to look like you *and* work for your lifestyle. Your friends should walk into your house and smile, because those few, well-chosen knickknacks on display are so "you" and because the bulletin board full of your child's (recent!) artwork is so fun to look at. And you're happy to entertain, because grabbing the chip-and-dip platter is easy, because you know just where it is. You already have hummus and pita and carrots in the fridge, because you've been "taking inventory." You are confident that your living room isn't a disaster because you've been doing a "last sweep" before bed. Your home isn't perfect, but it is organized enough that you can do things like spontaneously invite *anyone* over (not just the friend whose house is worse than yours!). You can relax because you are on top of your game: your bills are paid, the kids' school forms are filled out, and nothing is hanging over you.

Perhaps, right now, that all seems like a dream. If you are looking around your home and your life and seeing nothing but endless clutter and to-dos, you've come to the right place. This book will show you how making a few simple changes—thinking differently and starting new habits—will help you create a home that will support you and reflect the best of you, not embarrass and stymie you.

Embrace Your Wabi-Sabi

Wabi-sabi is a Japanese term meaning "the beauty of imperfection." Wabi-sabi is all around us, in the overflowing fruit bowl on our kitchen counter, the cashmere throw the art director tosses on the couch to make the impossibly perfect living room look more alive during a photo shoot. I love this concept because it's about beauty, and I won't lie, I love beauty. I am an aesthetic person; when I was a little girl my room was a mess, but my dollhouse had to be *just so*. But, as an adult, I realize that although I don't want to live in the chaos that was my childhood room, neither do I want to live in the stagnant perfection that was my dollhouse.

When our homes are basically orderly and functional, the chaos of a Lego castle under construction in the living room or a stack of books by the bedside aren't clutter; they are evidence of life being lived. And there is beauty in life being lived.

How This Book Works

In the first half, I introduce seven concepts that will help you shift perspective and define your goals:

1. Go with the FLOW.
2. Slow down, you move too fast.
3. Fresh eyes, fresh space.
4. Fear creates clutter.
5. Who are you now? Or, will you really use that bread maker?
6. Don't let paper push you around.
7. Better systems = less thinking.

A change in perspective may help you declutter and get organized, but how, you might ask, do I *keep* it that way? In the second half of the book, I teach you—whether you are truly disorganized and living in chaos or a type A perfectionist letting your overcomplicated systems rule your life—seven essential habits that, once instilled, will keep chaos and clutter at bay.

We are fortunate to be living at the beginning of the habit revolution, when neuroscience has unraveled the mysteries of how we form habits, but never before has this groundbreaking science been applied to one of the most important aspects of our lives: our homes. It isn't enough to know that you need to open and process your mail every night; you also need to know *why* you always dump it on the kitchen counter. Then you can come up with a personal strategy to change that behavior. This book is going to teach you how to reprogram yourself. Once you have come up with an alternative scenario (such as putting the mail on your desk) you need to concentrate on that one tiny change for one month, until you literally build a new neural connection in your brain. The habits I have chosen to include in this book seem small, but they are the cogs of a well-ordered life. By following my simple method, you can build foundational habits that will allow you the life you dream of: a life where you have time for things you are passionate about, instead of always feeling like you are fighting to keep up. I want you to feel in control, not overwhelmed.

I first experimented with consciously changing my habits in seventh grade. It wasn't my idea. I was struggling academically, and my mother and my teachers sat down and discussed what to do with me. Although I scored high on aptitude tests, my work was messy and inconsistent. My mother said that I spent hours doing homework, which surprised the teachers, who thought my work looked slapdash and hurried. They decided that I must not be working very effectively, and they came up with this solution: I was to take my mother's kitchen timer and set it for a half an hour. Then I was to do a single subject of homework. If I finished before the timer went off, I could get up and stretch, get a snack, whatever. If the timer went off before I finished the subject, I could take a break. After the break, I would reset the timer and sit back down to complete the subject or start the next one.

Immediately, and I mean the very first day, I cut my homework time in half. I still had terrible handwriting and a tendency to daydream, but working in small chunks was a revolution for me. On that day I learned one of the most important things I know: that I can focus on anything, no matter how difficult or dull, if I have to do it for only half an hour.

Clients tell me that they are overwhelmed, that they don't know where to start. Know this: there is no job, no mess, no chaos that can't be broken down into small chunks. The habits I will introduce are just that: small, focused ways to counteract the usual culprits that lead to disorganization— overbuying, lack of a plan, and lack of maintenance.

These habits will become the building blocks for your new, organized life:

1. Take inventory.
2. Block out time.
3. Do a last sweep.
4. Set limits on stuff.
5. Buy less but better.
6. Ten-minute maintenance.
7. Cultivate consistency.

If you're too busy and too stressed to deal, this book will help you. You don't have to let chaos keep you from the life you dream of. Close your eyes. Yes, right now. Imagine your perfect weekday evening. What does it look like?

Do you see yourself . . .

Feeding yourself and your family a healthy dinner and not resorting to takeout?

Not having to worry about whether you remembered to pay a bill on time (or where it might be)?

Easily pulling a favorite outfit (that's clean!) out of your closet and being excited to wear it the next day?

Having time to relax in a peaceful spot, read a favorite book, or let your mind wander?

All of those things are possible. You *can* come home every night to a home that doesn't nag you with lingering to-dos and instead brings you peace and serenity.

How Did My Home Get This Messy?

We get in ruts; after a while, we don't even really see our homes the way a newcomer would. We buy furniture, we decorate, and then we dump and pile and squish in more stuff that we don't know what to do with, so we ignore it. Soon that miscellany becomes a permanent fixture, almost part of the decor. Sometimes I am in a well-appointed apartment in an expensive zip code in Manhattan, and yet it is not a comfortable place to be. Although houses have gotten bigger and, in many ways, slicker—with custom closets, endless remodels, and stylish new furniture—they are often at the same time neglected. Like children who get too many toys but not enough attention, they seemingly have everything, but something is missing.

For example, I always know that there is an imbalance when I go into a home and there are bags of purchases lying around that have never been put away. That says to me that there is shopping happening that isn't about need. Sometimes my job is archaeological: I see evidence of fear, of rushing, of guilt, of aspiration. I recognize these things because I've done them all too.

How does this stuff accumulate? These days, we certainly seem to have less time, and less time at home in particular. For example, when I was a child, my mother stayed at home and never set foot in a gym. On the rare occasions I had after-school activities, I ventured there on my own. Compare that to today, when many families are under more pressure than ever, with two working parents who feel compelled to chauffeur their kids hither and yon and make it to the gym three times a week. It's no surprise that organizing falls to the bottom of the list. At the same time, if that weren't bad enough, it's never been easier to buy more for our homes. While we've been on the hamster wheel trying to keep up, the price of goods has been going down. Marketers' ability to reach out and grab us at our most vulnerable (sitting down with our omnipresent screens after a long day) and sell us more stuff we don't need has increased exponentially.

The good news is that you *don't* have to live like that. In fact, you have more control and more time than you may realize. To get organized, you don't have to totally reinvent your lifestyle: you are probably already doing a lot that *is* working. As the saying goes, it's not about working harder but working smarter.

I like metaphors. As I work with clients, I like to compare areas of their homes to places like delis and factories and nonprofit institutions in an effort to get them to think differently about their space. In his book *The Power of Habit*, Charles Duhigg makes the case that it is often a slight shift in perspective that allows us to change one habit, which then opens us up to being able to make other positive changes. He calls these habits "keystone habits," but you can't get there if you keep thinking the way you always have been.

I'll show you how to shift the balance, acquire less, and put just a little more time and effort into nurturing your living space, creating systems and routines that will keep your home healthy and functional. I want you to change the way you think. New habits are easier to acquire once you have shifted perspective, and new habits are how you are going to maintain your organization once and for all.

Form Does Follow Function

Throughout this book, I'll teach you how to develop habits and modes of thinking that will make organization absolutely effortless and seamless, so that you can spend less time being stressed and more time enjoying your home, your family, and your life. This book offers features you won't find anywhere else, a methodical, yet forgiving, system for developing the habits that will keep you organized:

A Groundbreaking, Science-Driven Approach: This method puts neuroscience to use to help people get and stay organized. Our homes are a reflection of our minds, and a scattered home can just as easily create a scattered mind. We'll work with your brain—rather than against it—to create a peaceful home and a peaceful mind.

A Proven Method for Maintaining Organization: Lots of people can get organized—it's *staying* organized that eludes them. This book addresses not just the steps of purging and reorganizing but also development of the habits that *maintain* that organization. I have successfully helped hundreds of clients develop the good organizational habits that result in lasting change.

An Anti-Perfectionist Philosophy: It's Okay to Have Stuff! For all the people who are "Kondo-ing" their drawers, there are others feeling less-than because they don't want to throw away 80 percent of their possessions—they just want to be able to find their kid's vaccination records. In my years of experience, I've found that perfectionism is a stumbling block for my clients, rather than something that makes them achieve more. This is a real book for real people. It isn't going to get your home featured in *House and Garden*, but it's going to help you get out of the house. On time. Appropriately dressed. Without forgetting a thing!

Getting Started

Before you begin, you might want to get a notebook. Don't buy one. You probably have a half-used one lying around somewhere—use that. Or take notes on your phone if you prefer. As you read, you may want to jot down notes about how these strategies apply to your situation. For example, if clothes are a big issue for you, may want to keep a clothing journal. Once you begin the habit-formation section, you may want to track your progress on a calendar or even on an app, but using the notebook as a journal can help you identify patterns when you are succeeding, or struggling, in your efforts to build these habits.

In her book *Reclaiming Conversation*, psychologist Sherry Turkle says that tracking data, while helpful, is really only the first step. To truly gain self-knowledge and effect change in ourselves, we need to construct a narrative. One of the most powerful tools in my organizational arsenal is to engage my clients in conversations about their struggles. I can fix a disorderly closet, and they can track how often they follow my advice to spend ten minutes per night on papers, but it is conversation that helps shift the way they think and opens up the space for change. For example, ask yourself: Why do I need it? When will I need it? Where is the logical place that I will remember to look for it? Can I rent it / borrow it / find it online? Can I let it go?

Journaling your story in a notebook will help you start that conversation with yourself. Often my clients say, "I never thought about it like that," or just, "I never thought about it." But here we are: it's time to think about it and it's time to change. Change comes from within.

If you are a visual person, you can make a photo journal, too. You can take some before-and-after shots to motivate yourself and create a Pinterest board of your progress if you like.

Change Is Just Around the Corner

Most of my clients live in New York City. In Manhattan, almost everyone, even the wealthy, has limited space. Living in small quarters makes people confront their clutter sooner (no attics or garages to hide it). But although New Yorkers may have particular challenges, the influx of too much stuff seems to be, if not a worldwide epidemic, at least a first-world epidemic. Whether you live in a sprawling home or a tiny apartment, the concepts in this book should be relevant to you.

You'll meet many of my clients in this book. I love them all: they are wonderful, creative, exuberant people. Of course, I've changed their names, and sometimes I've merged a few different people's stories to better elucidate my point. Working with them has taught me everything I know about organizing, and their stories animate this book. I hope you'll recognize yourself in some of them—and see that if they could do it, you can do it!

Coco, whose apartment had been so brimming with clutter she could barely walk through it, reclaimed her space. She was motivated and took my "homework" to heart. When I told her that if she spent just ten minutes per night on her paperwork, it would never pile up, she listened.

Over several organizing sessions we weeded, letting go of what she no longer needed and creating systems for what she did. Our work helped her to feel more in control and less anxious, which in turn helped her to be more productive.

She found the work we did on her paper-related clutter so inspiring that we flew through her clothes and household clutter. As Coco is an avid environmentalist, we found places to recycle her electronics and resell her unwanted clothing. After winnowing and organizing her clothes, they fit perfectly in her single closet and dresser. I told Coco that the key to continued success would be to get rid of one clothing item each time she acquired a new one, so that she wouldn't be back in the same boat in six months.

Once I explained the "rules" of organizing to Coco—like spending ten minutes per night on paper and maintaining the boundaries of her dresser and closet—she was able to develop those habits quite quickly. And I'm pleased to say that these days, nine years later, Coco is more organized than ever. She is also living in a much larger home with her new husband.

Do I think clearing her clutter and getting a handle on her finances led her to find true love and a bigger home? At the very least, I do believe that when you get rid of unneeded *stuff* you get rid of psychological as well as physical blockages. In truth, we don't want small, contained lives. We want a big life, one with multiple interests and passions and responsibilities. When you implement systems that are easy to maintain, you are building habits that are the foundation for your bigger, richer life—the life you want but have been too busy just staying afloat to achieve. Once you have that foundation, you create space for the things that really matter to you.

Okay. Take a deep breath. Let go of preconceived notions. Are you ready to change?

What's getting caught up in perfectionism versus being organized enough? I've created the chart below to help illustrate the difference.

PERFECTLY ORGANIZED	ORGANIZED ENOUGH
Scanning and digitally filing tax deductible receipts	Keeping a file of tax deductible receipts
Installing and maintaining a to-do app on your smartphone	Making a handwritten to-do list
Color coding your labeled files	Labeling your files
Sorting Legos by brick size into a special Lego storage container	Putting Legos in a bin

continues

continued

PERFECTLY ORGANIZED	ORGANIZED ENOUGH
Organizing socks in rows by color	Keeping all your socks together
Having all your glasses arranged in perfect rows	Having all your glasses in one cabinet
Attaching buttons to an index card with a description of the item and filing	Keeping extra buttons that come with clothes in a box
Photographing shoes and attaching the photograph to the shoe box	Labeling shoe boxes
Alphabetizing spices	Keeping all spices together
Alphabetizing a bookshelf within sections, or arranging spines by color	Organize bookcases by section: fiction, biography, sports, self-help, etc.
Keeping your in-box to zero	Keeping your e-mail in-box down to where you can see all your e-mails on your computer screen without scrolling
Rigidly adhering to a weekly menu	Having a general meal plan for the week
Clearing every paper off your desk before bed	Putting loose papers from around the common areas on your desk before bed
Buying perfectly matching labeled boxes from the Container Store to store office supplies in your office cabinet	Repurposing cardboard boxes with labels to store office supplies in your office cabinet

PART I

Getting Organized:
How to Think Differently

Does it seem like no matter how many times you try to tackle a cluttered area, you don't seem to be able to make any headway? Whether it's a perpetually overflowing closet or a desk awash in papers, over the years I've found that only a tiny shift in perspective is needed to get a client out of a rut and create lasting change. This first half of the book will address the most frequent stumbling blocks, like stagnancy, rushing, and fear, that lead us into chaos. I also want to make you think about your clutter on a deeper level. By asking yourself, "Who am I *now*?" you'll find clarity on what you really need to own. Once you've opened your mind and shifted your perspective, you'll be ready to build the habits described in the second half of this book. These habits are the secret to staying organized.

The idea of becoming *organized enough*, rather than *perfectly organized*, is asking you to change how you've thought about something in the past. The first section of this book introduces seven concepts that will help you to alter the way you think about organization, about your clutter, and about your space.

1. Go with the FLOW

In the first chapter, I introduce the concept of FLOW. Flow is a metaphor, because I want you to start thinking of your home as a living, breathing organism, but flow is also an acronym:

Forgive yourself
Let stuff go
Organize what's left
Weed constantly

These are the basic four steps that you'll use to organize everything from sweaters to documents. Getting organized isn't about buying new hangers or fancy bins; it's an inner journey.

2. Slow Down, You Move Too Fast

In the next chapter, we'll look at how the pace of modern society sets us up for clutter. Thanks to the speed at which goods are produced and the ease with which we can acquire them, we have become hamsters on a consumerist treadmill. Moreover, we are busy—too busy. Paradoxically, rushing doesn't make you more efficient. It makes you more frazzled, less focused, and more likely to make mistakes. Slowing down can actually help us simplify and prioritize. After all, we want our life to be better, not busier.

3. Fresh Eyes, Fresh Space

Familiarity breeds contempt. Sometimes we don't even see our homes anymore. Then we want to invite new friends over and suddenly . . . *oh no!* In this chapter, I suggest that you go through your home and see it as if for the first time. I challenge you to set a date and invite someone over for dinner. There is nothing that helps you see with fresh eyes like the prospect of some actual fresh eyes.

4. Fear Creates Clutter

Fear is also a major cause of clutter, and ignoring it just makes it worse. In this chapter we'll talk about a few different kinds of fear: fear of waste, financial fear, fear of litigation, perfectionist's fear, fear of missing out, and fear of loss. There are endless types of fear, but they can all be addressed in the same basic way: identify the fear, decide whether it's rational, and then take any steps we can to alleviate our anxiety. Finally, we have to practice moving forward in spite of fear. The best thing about facing your fears is that once you start to deconstruct them, they are usually pretty flimsy. Eliminating them just takes practice. After all, we're talking about sweaters and credit card bills, not lions and tigers.

5. Who Are You Now?

Self-knowledge is a beautiful thing. How can we know what we need, what to keep, and what to let go if we don't know who we are? We are changing all the time, and that's a good thing, but we need to be able to let go of our "past lives" as we move forward. We don't want to be tumbleweeds, accumulating more and more as we go. To fully be ourselves, we have to know who that is. Sometimes there is a little sadness that goes with letting go of objects that represent our past, but ultimately life is richer when we are truly in the life we have, not trying to keep one foot in the life we used to have or wished we had.

When I ask you to think about who you are, think about the circumstances of your life: "I'm a mom, a business owner, someone who loves to shop," and then dig deeper. What do you value *most*? For example, I aspire to have a beautiful home and to raise successful children: those are both things I want, but in the end I often sacrifice a perfect house in the interests of being a good mother, because when push comes to shove I value that more.

We all need to prioritize. For example, you may value protecting the environment, but, at the same time, you may find that having six different recycling containers and a compost bin in your small apartment just isn't the best use of your kitchen space. I aspire to buy everything made locally and organically, but I fail all the time, because in the end I often just can't spend that much on a T-shirt for a ten-year-old. It's okay not to do everything perfectly or 100 percent. What matters isn't so much what you value but that you are aware of how those values impact your choices.

6. Don't Let Paper Push You Around

I've devoted a special chapter to systems for dealing with paper, because it's the number 1 problem for so many of my clients, and possibly for you, too. Paper haunts us, follows us, and grows piles in corners of our homes when we aren't looking. We constantly feel like we have to "deal with it" or "sort it." Going back to our metaphor of our home as a body, we need to see paper as having a pathway: it comes in, it goes out. We need systems for it, because if we have to stop and think about each piece of paper coming in, well, that way lies madness, folks. We have to keep it simpler than that.

In this chapter, we discuss different kinds of paper—bills, invitations, forms—and present tried-and-true systems for managing them all. Lastly, because people now have digital clutter in addition to paper clutter, I explain the concept of a mirror system for your digital files. We'll see how creating simple systems can help us to establish routines that are neither cumbersome nor complicated so that we can stay on top of the paper without feeling overwhelmed by it.

7. Better Systems = Less Thinking

Paperwork isn't the only thing that benefits from a good system. Here, I introduce this fundamental truth: by really being present and putting in time up front, we can create systems for many areas of the home that we can use *without much thought* on a daily basis. In this chapter, we'll talk about different systems for everything from laundry to house-keeping. We will also look at how addressing fear and self-knowledge are part of the up-front work you need to do to create a great system. From allocating space to labeling to pathways, thoughtfully implementing systems will help you to create order and serenity in your living space.

Shake It Out

I hope I've already set your mind buzzing: "Slow down, really?" When I first work with clients, many are skeptical that this process will really work. They've tried to get organized before but failed, because the systems they set up were too labor intensive, because no one else in the house was on-board, or because they tried to do everything at one time. Before we can hope to establish the habits set forth in the second half of this book, I want you to open your mind, allow for the possibility of change, and get ready to alter your perspective. Think of this as the stretch before the marathon. It seems too easy to be very important, but in actuality it is key to your continued success.

CHAPTER 1

Go with the FLOW

We must begin thinking like a river if we are
to leave a legacy of beauty and life for
future generations.

—DAVID BROWER

I f you want to get organized, FLOW is the most important concept to know. You must think of your home as a
living thing: *things come in, things go out.* A room shouldn't
have stagnancy or blockages any more than your arteries or
intestines should. We want motion. FLOW is also an acronym for the basic organizational strategy that you can use to
tackle any area, room, or issue:

Forgive yourself
Let stuff go
Organize what's left
Weed constantly.

I have used the FLOW method to help clients with everything from e-mail management to garage storage. Crucially, the first step is forgiving yourself: you are human, and
you don't need to be perfect—you just need to be *organized*

enough. FLOW is your ultimate tool; memorize it, make it your screen saver, and put it up on the wall. You are going to use it!

1. Forgive Yourself

You are probably worried now. This seemed like a practical, sensible organizing book, but right here in the first chapter I'm getting all new-agey on you. Let me assure you that nothing could be further from the truth. I'm all about efficiency and doing what works. If beating yourself with a stick were useful, I would give you a stick. But it's not. In fact, it's the opposite.

Here are confessions I have heard from my clients when they first show me their homes: "I am sick." "I have a real problem." "I don't know what is wrong with me." These are not broken people but productive members of society, living in New York City, holding down good (often impressive!) jobs and responsibly paying their (often hefty!) mortgages. Nor, usually, are they people with terrible hoarding afflictions; they just need some help with order. That's normal. We all need help with something.

And yet they beat themselves up for having clutter. The problem with this kind of thinking is that it becomes self-fulfilling. You think "you are bad," which is different from acknowledging that you just have a few bad habits. *Bad habits, with proper diagnosis and some effort, can be changed.* Basically, this is the same advice psychologists give parents: make sure your children know that it is the *behavior* that is bad, not the child. Having a disorganized home does not mean you're sick or dysfunctional.

However it is that your home came to look the way it does, that's okay. You've paid thousands of dollars in late fees? Let it go. You can't find your passport? Breathe. Forgive yourself, and let's get on with the task of changing habits so we can solve the problem.

2. Let Stuff Go

"Let it go" is a phrase that I'd been overusing for years before the Disney song came out. A cornerstone of organizing, it's a concept that will show up in every chapter of this book. Almost all of us who are disorganized are disorganized because we have too much stuff. The antidote to too much stuff is to *let stuff go*. Bringing in less is even better, but that's advanced; before you can get to that (and you will) you have to part with some belongings. It may be painful, it may feel wasteful—but it is always and forever the most crucial step in organizing. Whether it's paper or clothes or pots and pans, chances are that you are going to have to let stuff go. That's okay! The more you discard, the easier step 3, organize what's left, is going to be.

Where to Start

Many times when I meet clients, they say, "I don't know where to start." I do. Start with something easy, the low-hanging fruit. Whether it's expired medicine or party favors, once you get that first rush when you chuck something in the garbage can, it's only going to get easier. It's also good to start where you will be able to make a visual impact pretty quickly, for example, a surface area like a desktop. You may find that it naturally leads you to a file cabinet, but even if you can't accomplish the entire inside of the file cabinet in one go, if you have made room for what was on the surface of your desk, you'll feel better.

And, while you are at it, remember to take some "before" pictures. When you finish, you can take some "after" shots. Not only will you be proud of your improvement, but also you can use the after pictures to help keep you on the beam.

Deciding What to Let Go and What to Keep

How do you decide what to let go of and what to keep? You ask yourself questions, and you answer them honestly.

If someone just walked into your house and started eating your food and watching your TV, you would ask them who they were and what they were doing there. The same goes for stuff that comes in the door. What is it, and what is it doing here? You may decide to let it stay, but, as you start this process, you have the right—in fact, an obligation—to question each and every item in your home.

You need to keep what you use, but this is key: you need to guard against having too many multiples. Let's say you have ten sets of napkins. You may, in fact, have used them all at one point—but you don't need ten sets of napkins. It will help if you can designate what drawer they should fit into, and that drawer will give you a boundary as to how many you can fit. With this in mind, you might decide, "Well, I rotate between the red and the blue for everyday, I use the white at Thanksgiving, and I really love the toile—but I can get rid of the other six sets."

Ideally you'll gather all of one category, be it napkins or sweaters or loose papers, into a pile, and you'll evaluate it all at once. You'll see that you have sixteen sweaters, and you'll realize that there are three or four you wear all the time. Next, you'll ask yourself, "Is it flattering? Is it in good condition? When was the last time I wore it? Do I love it? Is it me?" And even if you end up with seven, you've reduced your sweaters by more than 50 percent, and that is great.

As you evaluate what to keep, ask yourself:

Do I need it?
Do I use it?
Does it work?
Does it reflect me?
Do I love it?
How many of this item do I realistically need?

Now, did my kids' car seats sing to me? Hell no, but I kept them, because I love my kids. There will be items that you may not be passionate about, but you simply need. The point is to question why the item is there, then decide.

Getting It Out

There are many different avenues for letting go of stuff. You can give away, sell, recycle, or trash. The longer I do this job, the more environmentally aware I become, because I have seen an obscene amount of garbage bags go out the door. That said, if you have a lot to get rid of, throwing away is often the best course of action. Indeed, some people are just so happy to let go, they have no problem shoving it all into a big Hefty bag and tossing it!

Other people feel bad about throwing stuff out and feel better if they can pass it on to others who might be able to use it. This is ideal when it is easy, but it can also be a trap. I've been with clients who have a little bag of stuff for this person, a box for that charity, and a garbage bag for another charity—to the point where we have just created a lot more work and the clutter is now just sitting in bags by the front door instead of piled up around the house.

As with so many things, education and self-knowledge are key here. Find out which charity takes what and when they take it. Be honest with yourself about how easy it's going to be to take items to the various friends and charities you have in mind. If the answer is "not easy," return to step 1. Forgive yourself and throw that stuff out!

Similarly, although it is painful to give away things that cost a lot of money or that you perceive as valuable, sometimes it is just not worth the effort to get rid of it in some profitable way. When it comes time to sell your grandmother's tea set or the exercise bike you never use, just remember that your goal is to make your home more livable, *and that is of value as well.* Don't hold onto the tea set because you can't sell it for what you thought it was worth. Let it go to someone who will enjoy it. And frankly, if someone comes and picks up the exercise bike, you are winning even if you don't get a dime.

3. Organize What's Left

After you purge, then you get to organize. "But how? That's the part I don't get!" say my clients. My response: just like you did in kindergarten: "like with like."

In the process of letting go you have already begun to gather all like items together. Group everything in categories. This can be on a macro scale, like getting all the office supplies in your house into one spot—and then realizing that you don't have to buy paper for a year. Or it can be done on a micro scale, where you go through every little bit and piece in your desk drawer and put all the paper clips together in one pile and all the rubber bands in another. In the pantry, you put all the baking items together in one area, all the oils and vinegars together in another. In a file cabinet, you group all the bills in one folder, taxes in another.

People often don't realize how much duplication they have. You may have to do a second purge of excess items at this point to make the category fit into its allotted space. Really think about how many of an item you need. Do you have three ice buckets? Before you start to rationalize, "Oh, this one is a casual ice bucket, and that one is a fancy ice bucket, and . . . " ask yourself whether you really, truly use all of them often enough to justify their taking up space. What if you didn't have them—could you use a bowl instead? Likewise, do you really write notes often enough to justify an entire cabinet full of stationery? I didn't think so.

Once you know what you have, then you can think about containment. You'll need to designate a permanent space for those categories of items to live, keeping in mind that space is inherently limited. After all, no matter how neatly you fold, you can fit only so many pairs of socks in a drawer. Once again, you may need to go back to step 2 here and let it go if there is still too much in any category.

Only at this point can you decide if you need to buy a few organizing supplies. (Don't buy that stuff first!) You might see you need a plastic drawer for your backup toiletries or a box to separate your socks from your underwear. Always remember to measure the area first to make sure any boxes, drawers, or dividers will fit.

The point of containers is to keep items sorted so that you can access them easily. For example, if you have weeded down your jeans to two stacks in a drawer, you don't really need a divider to separate them. However, if you are organizing your bathroom supplies and the space under your sink is big, dark, and hard to access, you may want to buy some plastic drawers. I prefer stacking drawers rather than boxes whenever possible, because inevitably the item you want is going to be in the box at the bottom of the stack.

Sometimes a box is the right size, and if it's going in a closet or a bigger drawer where it doesn't need to be stacked, I just eliminate the lid—the lid only makes it harder for me to get what I need, not easier. Remember, your aim is to simplify your life, not be a photo shoot for *Real Simple*. And, by the way, I've been on photo shoots, and there is *always* a big pile of stuff outside the frame waiting to go back in. 'Cause real life is not a magazine!

4. Weed Constantly

This is the maintenance part of FLOW. You've let stuff go, you've organized—and you don't want to backslide. Remember that your home is a living, breathing thing, like a garden. You must constantly weed and winnow items because, with no effort on your part, it will always be growing. Stuff accumulates. Whatever category seems to grow on its own in your house—clothes, toiletries, toys—that's where you have to focus your weeding energy.

Keep a dedicated bag in the closet or a box in the garage for items that need to be passed on. Make sure that every member of the household knows that that is where stuff to be given away hangs out until you can get it to the thrift

The Container Store Is Not the Answer

A word on the Container Store. People love this place, and, because I am an organizer, people assume that I love it too. I understand the appeal, and I am not immune to it: it is soothing to see all that order, all those neat rows of boxes promising to end the chaos you left back at home. But it's an illusion.

When I visit clients' homes, I typically enter the scene after they have made several attempts to organize on their own. Often these attempts involved a trip to the Container Store, and there are many attractive boxes full of disorganized stuff to prove it. Usually there are leftover boxes after we purge. What a waste!

The Container Store will not magically solve your clutter problem—it's a resource. Once you have done the steps of FLOW, measured your space, and figured out exactly what container shape (deep? shallow? rectangular? square?) is necessary, then the Container Store is where you can pretty much find whatever it is that you have decided you need.

But you can always go without these pretty containers. My mother never set foot in the Container Store, and she was totally organized. She used an empty safety-match box for rubber bands, the bottom of a necklace box for pencils, and toilet-paper rolls for cord control. Recently I was with a client who had repurposed the inside of a chocolate box to sort earrings, a trick she learned from her mother. The truth is, any box will do.

No box or bin will organize your stuff for you; you have to do it yourself. The box or bin, as the store's name suggests, will simply *contain* what you have organized. It isn't the Organization Store. Organization isn't a product you can buy. It is an action you do.

store or wherever you are taking it. Make weeding part of your rhythm and routine.

Where are there blockages in your home? Just because you can shut a cabinet door doesn't mean the area isn't blocked. If you have to spend a lot of time rearranging your refrigerator to put groceries away, you have a blockage. If you can't see what you have in your pantry, you have a blockage. What can you let go of?

Again, tackle one small area at a time, whether it's a pile of papers on the countertop or an overstuffed utensil drawer. Empty it out, and as you look at each item, ask yourself,

- Do I need it?
- Does it belong here?
- Does it fit who I am now?
- If I let it go, will I end up replacing it?

If the answer is no, you know what you have to do.

FLOW in the Kitchen

Kitchens are hubs of living, the heart of the home. They are also caches of used-once items like baseball mitt–shaped cake pans and fondue pots, along with piles of mail that somehow landed and got stuck there. It's easy to see why we would want FLOW in our kitchen. Who wants cabinets full of expired cans and stuff we never use? You want your kitchen to be a healthy place where you can cook and come together as a family.

When I first met Leslie, she had just given birth to her third child and was about to return to her job as a television producer. Energetic and driven, Leslie excelled in every area of her life: She was a hands-on mom, a devoted wife, and a successful career woman firing on all cylinders. In the last weeks of her maternity leave, we whipped through her apartment, getting rid of accumulation and stagnancy and making room for her new daughter.

In her kitchen, Leslie had every specialized utensil Williams-Sonoma ever thought of, as well as myriad gourmet ingredients gathering dust in her pantry. Although she loved to cook, between working long hours and spending time with her children, she wasn't really cooking elaborate, dinner party–worthy meals these days.

In addition, in Leslie's home there were a lot of people using the kitchen. There was Leslie; her husband, Dan; and their nanny, Fern; as well as her sons, who were beginning to be independent enough to get their own snacks and pour themselves juice. Problem was, Dan was tall and tended to shove groceries in on high shelves. Fern had carved out her own corner for the stuff she used for the kids, and Leslie felt like the almonds were in a different spot every time she looked. Having so many cooks and shoppers and snackers in the kitchen made it vital to designate a place for everything and then get everyone on board so that everything would stay in its place. A few strategically placed labels (*Snacks, Plastic Cups*, etc.) also helped keep everyone on track.

I urged her to embrace the wonderful, rich life she had now and to let go of the past life she was clinging to in the form of pâté terrines and escargot dishes. For Leslie, "forgive yourself" meant accepting that she wasn't going to be Martha Stewart—at least not at this stage of her life—and being okay with that. It was a huge step for her. As we worked our way through her kitchen cabinets, our aim was to make the space functional, so that, when she was rushing in the morning or trying to prepare dinner after a long day, her kitchen supported her rather than fought her.

Then, it was time to let go. We started in the higher reaches of the cabinets, where Leslie had stashed rarely used wedding gifts. Did she really need two ice buckets? And how about that pâté terrine? She'd used those gifts once upon a time, but as a mother pushing forty, she had become more interested in eating healthfully and didn't really see herself making terrine even after her children got older and she had time for labor-intensive projects. By winnowing the upper cabinets, she now could easily access the wedding gifts that she *did* use, albeit not daily, like the chip platter and the blender.

When we moved into the lower cabinets, Leslie confronted another issue. Her husband worked near an excellent baking store that sold every kind of specialty pan imaginable. Over the years she had frequently shopped there before her sons' birthday parties, and as a result she had accumulated cake pans in the shape of baseball mitts, Mickey Mouse, and Darth Vader, to name but a few. The problem with novelty items is that the novelty wears off. A year later, most kids are on to something different. I encouraged Leslie to let go of the specialized pans and to keep the sheet pans and round cake pans. She could decorate the cakes in whatever theme she liked, but her future cakes could be round or rectangular. No more novelty cake pans.

One idea I like to impart to my clients is what I call "the power of one." A funny thing happens when you just have one of something, whether it's a hair elastic or a water bottle (or even a child!): you are aware of where it is at all times. When you have multiples of everything, they are everywhere, underfoot, overflowing; in contrast, having less means fewer objects to keep track of and store. Everyone has an excuse: "We need extra water bottles in case we lose them." "This carrot peeler is just so great I bought three in case one wears out." Trust me, you are better off with one. One water bottle, one carrot peeler. When you organize, you must confront your duplication and let stuff go.

At Leslie's, we weeded out more common kitchen clutter culprits: extra mugs and accumulated plastic cups. Having done this, the remaining glasses and cups now fit onto two shelves, and it was easy for everyone in the house to see exactly where they were stored. Now, when Leslie's son George wanted his favorite Mets cup, he didn't need to shout to his mother in another room. It also meant that if Dan emptied the dishwasher, he could tell where the glasses were supposed to go. This made everyone's life easier.

Last, we looked at Leslie's pantry. She did a lot of cooking in her relatively small New York kitchen, but she was giving up valuable eye-level storage space to keep exotic ingredients that she didn't really use any more. We let go of ancient coconut milk from a flirtation with Thai cuisine, spirulina powder that she couldn't stand, and the ginger candies she'd used to combat nausea during her last pregnancy. Out went dried beans that she never had time to deal with and expired tapioca that she couldn't remember buying. Instead, we made room for the items she was using now, which had been cluttering the counter: lunch boxes for her sons and the protein bars they liked to snack on.

By using the steps of FLOW, Leslie was able to transform her kitchen. First, she *forgave* herself for not being Martha Stewart, then she *let go* of those terrines and expired coconut milk. She also let go of unnecessary duplicate items. We *organized what was left* by grouping like items together and designating dedicated areas for them, including creating priority space for things she grabbed often. Once she saw how great it looked, she was inspired to *weed constantly* to keep her kitchen feeling healthy and orderly.

The Organized Enough Kitchen

- Store everyday glasses close to the fridge or sink, preferably in a cabinet that can be accessed without disturbing the cook.
- Put everyday dishes close to the stove for easy serving, and use high cabinets for less often used and specialty items (teapots, serving dishes).
- Group your cookware into sections: cooking, baking, and prep (mixing bowls, graters, colanders).
- Organize pantry items into a few general categories: pasta/grains, oils/vinegars, spices, tea/coffee (hot chocolate and sweeteners could go here too), snacks, and baking. Again, try to put coffee near the coffee maker and snacks in an easy-access place, while baking can typically be farther up because it is less often used.

FLOW in a Child's Room

Let's look at how FLOW works in another area of the home. I've been teaching my children the concept of FLOW since they could walk. For many people, children are the biggest obstacle to getting organized, as well as the most important reason to *be* organized. No matter how vigilant you are, kids seem to be clutter magnets, and a lot of it isn't their fault. They aren't the ones ordering party favors from Oriental

Trading Company. They didn't decide that everyone who participates in Pee-Wee Soccer should get a trophy. They didn't come up with a brilliant marketing scheme for Legos that ensured every kid in America would "need" thousands of dollars' worth of Legos before they graduated from high school.

Love the Kid You Have

My client Becky was clearly embarrassed as we went through the random piles on the floor of her son's room. It was like an archaeological dig into the twenty-first-century American boy: Legos, electronics, baseball cards, a gazillion Silly Bands. It was a mess. But for me it was great: I knew we were going to make a huge, noticeable change, because so much of the stuff was garbage. Ryan's room was a study in stagnancy. High shelves were full of books he'd outgrown, while current books were stacked on the floor. Lower shelves were full of old Legos and Beyblades, even though he had now graduated to Erector Sets and Xbox. There was also the usual assortment of complete and utter garbage from birthday party gift bags and giveaways: plastic key chains, lousy whistles, pooping pigs (okay, we kept the pooping pig). But there was a lot of stuff that if I were queen, wouldn't exist in the first place.

As we put boxes of unopened puzzles and never-built Lego sets into a carton for the Salvation Army, Becky had to *forgive herself.* She couldn't believe how much money she had spent on stuff that Ryan had never used. Workbooks with one page done, dried-out poster paints: the room was a shrine to her hopes for her son. I had to point out to her that though he hadn't used the workbooks, he still was doing well in school, and just because he preferred video games to jig-saw puzzles didn't mean she'd failed. Part of Becky's process was realizing that if she wanted to reduce waste and clutter, she was going to have to start buying for the kid she had, not the kid she aspired for him to be.

Becky and I started on the high shelves with the books Ryan had outgrown. It's always good to start in an area you know will be easy. That way you make some space right off the bat and you begin to have a feeling of accomplishment. Becky had a new nephew, so we put the not-too-chewed-up board books in a box for him. Other books went in boxes for charitable donation or recycling, depending on their condi-tion. New or rarely used games and puzzles that she thought Ryan had outgrown or just didn't like also went into the charity box. Once we got into it, Becky was shocked at how easy it was to *let stuff go*.

However, when we got to the Legos, which were every-where, Becky hit a roadblock. Even though her son wasn't into Legos anymore, it bothered her to throw them out be-cause she realized she had spent hundreds (possibly thou-sands!) of dollars on them over the years. Eventually we wrangled all the Legos into a few plastic bins, and Becky listed them for sale on her neighborhood parents' LIST-SERV. Although she made only a fraction of what she had spent, she felt better selling them, and the person who bought them was thrilled. Sometimes people get stymied be-cause they want to let something go but they aren't sure how or where to dispose of it. This is something that gets easier with practice. With many years of experience, my brain is filled with the rules and regulations of all sorts of New York City charities, but you are probably going to have to go on-line and make some calls at first. The good news is, once you know the rules in your area, you can make donating or selling unwanted stuff part of your routine.

Becky and I made quick work of the garbage from birthday parties—pitching most of it and keeping a little stash in a box her son had made in kindergarten that Becky was reluctant to part with. We moved on to the papers, which was slower going. Becky kept a few funny examples of Ryan's writing and some of his artwork. We put them aside, and Becky made a note to purchase an inexpensive portfolio to save his best artwork and a binder with pocket folders for each year where she could keep a few mementos, like the writing samples and awards, in addition to Ryan's report cards. Two hours later, there was nothing on the floor but a box of old schoolwork that Becky didn't feel the need to keep but wanted Ryan to weed through and see whether there was anything he wanted to save.

Becky and I then *organized what was left:* books on shelves, building sets and electronics in baskets on a lower shelf, art and school supplies in the desk drawer. We had even left enough space in the desk for the schoolwork waiting in the box, but she knew Ryan would throw most of it out. We took a few minutes to get file folders from Becky's desk and made labels for each of Ryan's fifth-grade classes. Becky wasn't sure he would want to use them, but she liked the idea of giving him a structure that he could use if he did.

Becky was amazed by what we accomplished in four hours. The lesson for Becky and Ryan was that they didn't need to wait for the clutter to become a crisis. Now, they needed to develop the habit of *weeding constantly.* Becky could help by guiding Ryan through a twenty-minute purge anytime the room looked like it was becoming cluttered again. They decided that, at a minimum, at the end of every semester they would go through Ryan's school papers and dispose of most of them. By cultivating the habit of weeding, Becky was sure she and Ryan would be able to keep chaos at bay and the room functioning in a healthy way.

The key to corralling children's clutter long term is the same as for pantry items, paper, clothes, or anything: make sure you are creating outgoing pathways to balance what is coming in. Every year before birthdays and Christmas, I get my children to do a toy purge. Do they give away the same volume that they receive? Not at all, but it is a habit worth instilling and an idea (stuff is coming in, so stuff should go out) that I want to reinforce.

The Organized Enough Kids' Room

- Make sure kids can reach what they use most.
- Keep storage simple. They won't put it away if it is too complicated.
- Use bins on a regular bookshelf so that, as kids grow, you won't have to replace the furniture.
- Label, label, label: from clothing drawers to toy bins, labeling helps kids know where things go.
- Set up a binder for report cards and keepsakes to be kept by year.
- Purchase a basic, inexpensive portfolio to keep the best of their elementary school art.

Getting in the FLOW

The concept of FLOW can be used in any area of your home; the process of decluttering is really about unblocking. We aren't setting up a model house where nothing ever moves. Our homes should be extensions of ourselves, and hopefully that means they are evolving all the time.

Beginning the project of becoming *organized enough* by forgiving yourself is key. Being full of self-recrimination and judgment is a waste of time and energy. I want all of your energy focused on building new habits—so forgive yourself and get ready to move on!

Because you are about to start letting stuff go, take a few minutes to think about, or possibly even contact, the places where you can donate. Does your local charity accept stuffed animals? Clothes? Housewares? What are their hours? Do they accept donations any time? Do they pick up? Does your local library accept books? Is there stuff you want to sell on-line? Is it worth it?

If you are throwing stuff away, and you probably will be, research the rules in your community. Are there particular days for "big" garbage? Are you going to need to take stuff to the dump? Are there rules about disposing of paint or electronics? Almost all of the answers are available online, so spend a few minutes investigating before you start filling up black garbage bags with old files only to discover that paper needs to go into clear blue bags.

Throughout the book I'll continue to spotlight different areas of the home, with examples of how to actually organize what you do keep, but it's good to remember that, at the most basic level, all organizing is just grouping like items with like, in one location. Two questions to always ask yourself when organizing your space are "Is it logical?" and "Is it accessible?" It doesn't matter how well I fit a bunch of stuff into the top of your closet—if you don't remember it's there and you can't access it, I haven't really helped you very much.

The second half of this book will be devoted to the process of maintaining your organization. No matter how organized you make your space, it won't stay that way if you don't have good habits. We will think about weeding in different ways: as a way to manage inventory, as a maintenance tool, and as a way to stay within the boundaries you have defined for yourself. But at its most elemental, it is all weeding. Your home is a garden. You need to ensure it doesn't become overgrown, and you want its beauty to shine.

Remember . . .

Forgive yourself (don't get caught up in self-recrimination).

Let stuff go (pass it on, recycle it, or purge it—it's good to get it out).

Organize what's left (group like with like in an accessible, logical place).

Weed constantly (resist the creep of more stuff and maintain boundaries).

CHAPTER 2

Slow Down,
You Move Too Fast

There is more to life than increasing its speed.

—GANDHI

I can still hear my mother's voice, over and over in my mind: "Slow down, Amanda." My mother had my number. From very early on in my childhood, she would point out when I was rushing through, making careless errors in my math homework or leaving words out when I copied over my history essay (oh, the difference a computer would have made!). My mother was always urging me to do things properly, and she promised me that in the long run it would save time.

I'm sad to say it took me years and quite a bit of yoga to realize that she was right. My mother was the least Zen person I've ever known, and yet she understood that, whatever task you do, you need to fully commit to it. Or, to steal a phrase, you need to *be here now*. Contrary to what you might think, rushing does not improve efficiency. It stresses you out, distracts you, and makes you more prone to errors. Good upfront planning saves time and effort down the road—this is an obvious step, yet it's so often ignored.

While I am by nature a fast person, my husband is by nature a slow and extremely methodical person. What can I say? Opposites attract. Although I find Gary's slower pace somewhat maddening, I also respect it, because I have seen the benefits. Before we were married, Gary was managing a large and bustling restaurant on Manhattan's East Side. Occasionally I would fill in as a hostess. I remember waiting, tapping my foot with a couple eager to be seated, while Gary slowly studied the map of the room and decided what table I should take them to. All night long, I had to practice my deep breathing to avoid snapping at him.

The following night I was working with Gary's coworker, Jeff, as the maître d'. Jeff was like me, short, intense, quick. Customers would come in, and two seconds later I'd be heading through the restaurant to seat them. Great.

Except that it wasn't great, because more than half of the people didn't like the first table Jeff sent them to. This was a huge, crowded restaurant, and there were no walkie-talkies, so it was a huge deal that I had to repeatedly go back and forth. I learned that night that there was a method behind Gary's "slowness" and that there was something I could learn from it. Taking time up front ended up saving time down the line.

Rapid Consumption Creates Clutter

Early in my organizing days, I worked with one client who had several children, a big career, and a lot of stuff. I remember opening bags of purchases for her children that had never been opened. It struck me as ironic: she'd rush out during her brief lunch break and buy things for her kids that they didn't really need, and now she was spending half of a personal day with me to fill bags of toys for donation. And that's not even talking about the cost of the toys or my services, or the schlepping involved in getting all that stuff to the thrift store.

I'm not naïve; I know that it wasn't an even trade. Leslie couldn't have the job she had and spend more time at home. But sometimes it does seem like a hamster wheel to me: we rush to make money, we rush to buy, we rush to organize our possessions, and then we start over.

The rise of Internet shopping has not helped the situation. An idea of something we might want flicks through our head (possibly because an ad briefly appears on our screens), and minutes later that something has begun its journey to us. It's too easy. It's too fast. And it adds up to clutter.

So it makes me ask, How can we slow it down?

I'm not alone or unique in feeling that the speed at which we live today is hurting us. In fact, a whole "slow" movement has sprung up in resistance to our breakneck pace and is spreading—rapidly.

The first slow movement began, decades ago, as a protest against a McDonald's planned for Rome's Piazza di Spagna. The protesters considered the proliferation of American fast food a threat to the Italian way of life, from the local farmers to how people ate. They believed that the Italian way of eating was cultural and that by succumbing to the American grab-n-go mentality, they would lose a part of their culture. The first protest was in 1986, and in 1989 they signed the Slow Food Manifesto in Paris.

Since then, all kinds of slow movements have sprung up. One that is particularly interesting to me is the Slow Fashion movement, which focuses on buying locally made and sustainably sourced fashion, as opposed to mass-produced clothing. With so many clients who have too many clothes, I can't help but think selecting a few better-made pieces is the way to go.

Or, even—not buying new clothes at all. Starting with the belief that adding *time* to *impulse* would curb her urge to buy clothes on the Internet, author and illustrator Sarah Lazarovic created the book *A Bunch of Pretty Things I Did Not Buy*. In this little gem, Lazarovic shares how she challenged herself to not buy any clothes for a year, and when she had the urge, she drew them and wrote about the experience instead. I love that by slowing down the process she not only resisted the impulse to buy a bunch of clothes she really didn't need but she also produced a beautiful, creative work.

Toiletries Take Over

One client, Carol, is a television personality. She is gorgeous and busy, and she travels frequently. We first met when I helped her move into her New York apartment, and on that visit it was apparent her toiletries and makeup were out of control. They filled two large medicine cabinets and several shelves in the linen closet. We purged, we married what we could, and we put backups in categories (shampoos, body lotions, face creams, and so forth) . . . and there was *still* a lot.

When I asked Carol how she had ended up with so many toiletries, she confessed that, because she was frequently sent out of town at the last minute, she was always rushing, so she didn't always pack as carefully as she should. Moreover, because she was on air, looking great was part of her job. Unlike when she was in New York, she didn't always have a hair and makeup person on the road. A common scenario: she would arrive at her hotel and realize she had forgotten something, so she'd race to the nearest drugstore to get it. Often, she bought other things she didn't need on those little excursions.

In addition, being a celebrity meant she was often given free things—expensive perfumes, fancy skin creams, and other luxury beauty products. Because she was so busy, she didn't really take the time to integrate these freebies, she just added them to her already overflowing stock.

All the overbuying and free samples created an avalanche of toiletries. It was incredible how much real estate they were taking up in her spacious bathroom and linen closet.

No one—*no one*—needs five deodorants, three eye-makeup removers, or six blushes. When we analyzed the problem, we were able to create a system. Because Carol traveled so frequently, it was reasonable for her to maintain a prepacked toiletry kit. In fact we created two: one for one- or two-night jaunts and another for longer trips. Now, before she left town, she would just need to refill the containers that were already packed with her usual products, and she was set. No thinking, no stress, and no forgetting something essential and having to buy on the fly.

As we weeded, Carol also threw out many of the freebies she had been given, and she realized that she could be more conscious about what she kept from the start. By spending a minute really looking at a gift, she might think: "I don't really need this," and pass it on to one of the young interns working in her office. She needed to *slow down* that moment instead of reflexively tossing the gifts in her bag to take home.

Carol and I also discussed her instinct to keep the freebies, despite already having plenty. Though Carol didn't grow up poor, she wasn't from a rich family, either. No matter how much money she makes now, there is always a part of her that is amazed when she is given, for no reason, expensive products. Her initial instinct is to keep them, because they are valuable. Once we talked about it, Carol could see that these freebies were taking up even-more-valuable space in her apartment, and, most valuable of all, they took up her time as she tried to sort through them.

In talking about her shopping habit, Carol found that some of her buying had been a comfort mechanism. Traveling was stressful, and drugstores are identical wherever you go. There was something familiar and soothing about running off to buy (yet another) jar of makeup remover and roaming the aisles picking up sundries. After she realized this, she understood that she could create healthier routines to make her feel at home when she traveled.

Once we had revamped Carol's travel system and talked about her triggers, she felt confident that she would be able to avert another avalanche of toiletries from taking over her space.

If your medicine cabinet and vanity are overflowing, take a minute and sit down with the garbage can. Is there stuff that is expired? Do you have duplicates? Remember the steps of FLOW. Try to put the things you use daily in the easiest-access spot, and take note of how much duplication you have. In the upcoming months, really try to be aware of when and how you buy these items so that you can change your behaviors so that you don't end up with so much excess.

Slow Down and Make a Plan

Joan was another victim of rushing. An elegant woman nearing her eighth decade, Joan had done it all: a huge career, wonderful kids and grandkids, several fabulous homes. She had traveled the world and now devoted her retirement

The Organized Enough Medicine Cabinet

- Create zones for categories of items: *Daily Use, Face, Teeth, Nails, Hair, Summer* (sunblock and bug spray).
- Keep tiny tubes (like bacitracin or lip balm) in a votive holder or some other small jar to make them neat and easy to access.
- Move rarely used and heat-sensitive items to another location, like a linen closet.
- Make beauty routines simple: resist five-step regimens and specialty creams.
- Keep a list on your phone or a notepad so that you know what you need, rather than guessing when you are at the store and ending up with duplication.
- Be honest with yourself. Either throw stuff out or commit to finishing it up before you buy new. Don't keep the shampoo that is too smelly hanging around if you aren't using it.
- If the cabinet starts looking cluttered, check expiration dates and see what can go.

years to charitable causes. When I first met Joan, I wondered how I could help her. Her apartment seemed perfect, and she seemed like a model of efficiency. Once we got started, however, I began to see that there was work to be done, and much of it was catch-up from fifty years of moving too fast.

What bothered Joan particularly was the disorganization of her photographs. Pictures from her entire life, and those of her children and grandchildren, were squirreled away throughout her apartment—a box here, a shopping bag there, some in files and some in piles. We gathered all the photos together and sorted them into categories, and today she is still in the process of creating albums. It has been a monumental project, and, in retrospect, it's easy to see how it could have been made simpler.

I imagine that back in 1975, as a newly divorced parent with three school-age children at home and beginning her career, worrying about organizing her photos wasn't at the top of Joan's list. Yet she took pictures, dropped off the film (that's what you did in 1975), and picked up the prints at the developer. So it isn't so outrageous to think that she could have taken one more little step—after all, she is a very efficient person. If at some point she had created the most rudimentary filing system, it would have saved hours, even days, when it eventually came time to make the albums.

When we are caught up in our lives and the pressing demands of family and work, it's easy to ignore the "little" projects. Yet, often, putting on the brakes first—slowing down to really be conscious of what you are doing—can lead to tiny

---

Organized Enough Photos and Memorabilia

- Keep it all in one location. A box is fine; just have one spot.
- Date your items as you go. If you ever do get around to making that album or scrapbook, it will be far easier if you have dated them along the way.
- If you have multiple children and are storing their drawings and projects, make sure you put their initials on each item. You may think you can tell the difference, but I'm here to tell you . . . you may forget!

actions that yield big payoffs later. What if Joan had paused to ask herself, "Why am I shoving this shopping bag of photos onto the top shelf of my coat closet?" Just asking that question could have led her to think, "Gee, I should put all my photos in one spot," or even, "I'd better just write the date on these." Before you stash something temporarily for a project you'll get to "later," step back, slow down, and make a plan for it first. Even the simplest plan is better than no plan at all.

Putting on the Brakes

So here is my manifesto: slow down, be a careful consumer, and be fully in whatever moment you are in. Here are some ways to put that into action:

- Try the Sarah Lazarovic method and add time to your impulse. Never buy something the first time you see it. Sit with it. Ponder it. With any luck, you'll get over it.
- Take your campaign to social media. Whenever you resist an impulse purchase, share it on social media with *#Resist*. Sometimes it's easier to change if we know others are on the same journey or at least supporting our attempts.
- When you do buy something, make it special. Take the time to unwrap it as soon as you get home, cut off the tags or wash off the stickers and find a place for it. If you just toss the bag in a pile, you probably didn't really need it, whatever it is. If it's replacing something else, get rid of what it is replacing.
- Look at what there is too much of in your house. Ask yourself, "How did it come to be there? When

did I buy/acquire it? Can I change that habit or eliminate that scenario?"

- Work on letting your style evolve over time. Resist purchasing articles of clothing just because they are inexpensive.
- Savor your stuff. Eat breakfast on your good dishes. Wear your favorite dangly earrings. Don't hoard for another day. The day is today. If you love it enough to keep it, then use it.

Sometimes the wise course of action is counterintuitive. By slowing down, even when we feel so rushed, we may realize that some of the tasks we "have" to get done aren't important at all. By being more deliberate and less reactive, we save time in the long run.

Remember . . .

Slow down, be thoughtful.

Add time to impulse in order to resist unnecessary purchases.

Take the time to make a plan—it will save time in the long run.

CHAPTER 3

Fresh Eyes, Fresh Space

The real voyage of discovery consists not in seeking
new landscapes, but in having new eyes.

—MARCEL PROUST

Familiarity breeds contempt. Sometimes we don't even notice our rooms anymore. Then we want to invite friends over, and we suddenly realize that the house is a disaster. One of the biggest keys to my success, and I think the success of any organizer, is that we bring fresh eyes to a space that may have been evolving organically but not always logically. Get an actual pair of "fresh eyes" in the form of a friend or organizer, or simply walk through your home as if you were a guest, and suddenly you will "see" all the niches where clutter lurks. Try it. It works.

When I first visit clients' homes or offices, I always ask them to give me a tour. I don't just want to see the disorganization, I'm also interested in what's working. As they walk me through and give me the rundown of different areas—"Somehow we always have a pile of mail on the kitchen table," or, "My daughter keeps her ballet stuff in this tote bag, and she always knows just where to get it"—I begin to make certain observations:

- **Stagnancy:** Are there areas that are dusty? Things that look like they have just been sitting there for a while?
- **Randomness:** Is the flashlight in the same cabinet with the chewing gum and the salsa? Why? There might be a good reason, but more likely it just got tossed in there in a rush of "straightening up" and never made it back to the utility closet.
- **Overflow:** Are some closets bursting at the seams? Do shelves have double layers of books? Are there toys on the floor?
- **Space:** Is there extra space at the top of the closet? Under the kitchen counter? Are there cabinets being underutilized or storing stuff that doesn't fit well?
- **Logic:** Does the layout of stuff make sense? Could a guest find a coffee cup in two tries? Would a new babysitter instinctively know where to find a change of clothes for the baby?

Sometimes people confuse squirreling away with organizing. "Squirreling" is when you put something "away" in any tiny crevice you can find—not necessarily in a logical, well-thought-out place, just out of sight. To me this is the opposite of organizing. Okay, I'll just say it: to me this is *cheating.*

Fresh eyes is about cultivating the capacity to really see what we have, what our spaces look like, and how they can be optimized.

Fresh Eyes in the Living Room

Shared living spaces often become dumping grounds that harbor stagnant piles of unopened mail and dusty knick-knacks, and Deena's place was no exception. Because the desk in her office area was covered in papers, it was largely unusable, so more stacks of paperwork had migrated to the kitchen table and the living room. Her two sons had staked out permanent territory in the living room with their schoolbooks and games, while sentimental clutter gathered dust on the bookshelves. Deena knew her apartment was cluttered, but she couldn't see how or where to start getting organized.

Deena had several jobs. She worked at as a reading specialist in a school, which was great because it meant her schedule was the same as her sons', but she also did some freelance translation work from home to bring in extra money. Her sons were excellent students but not very neat. Each night by the time they had eaten dinner and done their homework, very little time was left to straighten up before bed.

Bringing my fresh eyes to her space, I approached each area and asked some questions to help Deena focus. You can ask yourself these questions as you identify clutter throughout your home:

- What is this pile?
- When did it land?
- How did it grow here?
- Does this stuff have a home? If so, where does it belong? If not, what is the obstacle?
- Do you even need it?

First, we approached Deena's desk. Because it was such a mess, it had become her habit to do paperwork at the kitchen table, which then needed to be cleared off before dinner. She would sweep what she was working on into a pile, which she then deposited on the desk. And so the vicious cycle continued.

We got rid of tons of paper (more on this in Chapter 6) and tried to make her desk a space where she could actually pay her bills, not just dump them. This was key because it would make dinnertime easier: by committing to doing paperwork at her desk and reserving the kitchen table for eating, Deena was not only making dinner preparations less stressful, she was also stopping those piles before they began.

How had the problem started? We discovered that one reason Deena didn't like her desk area was that it was dark. Once we had gone through shopping bags of papers that had accumulated around the desk (and put 99 percent of what was in them into recycling), Deena realized that she could easily fit a standing lamp next to the desk. It was such a simple solution, but she'd just never taken the time to think through her desk issues. Talking about them with another person allowed her to see the problem with fresh eyes.

In the living room, Deena also often did her freelance translation work at a table under the window. At first this area struck me as a great place for her sons to do homework, but Deena said that her sons always did homework on the couch. In addition, she often did this work on weekends when her sons were out playing sports or with their dad.

The table by the window had a great view of the river, and Deena enjoyed sitting there with her laptop. We decided that because the work didn't really require any papers, just a few well-thumbed dictionaries, Deena would continue doing her translation work in that spot. But since she usually paid bills and did other paperwork on weeknights while the boys were doing their homework, it made sense for those tasks to be done at her desk. We took the time to move any non-translation work to her newly organized desk and integrate it into her newly organized files.

When I first saw Deena's bookcases, crowded with dusty tchotchkes and double layers of books, I thought that de-cluttering them was going to be hard. It turned out I was wrong. Deena just hadn't *seen* these objects or thought of them in years. Our goal was to have nothing overflowing on the shelves, which meant losing 50 percent of the tchotchkes and allowing only one row of books per shelf. We filled two cartons with books in a matter of minutes and more than half of the knickknacks went out, many directly into the gar-bage. There was also stuff that Deena wanted to keep but that could be grouped with other like items and relocated, such as unframed pictures, which she put in a drawer where she had stored some empty photo albums and other old pic-tures. She also moved coasters to the coffee table, which made much more sense than having them on the bookshelf.

Although the edges of the room were Deena's prob-lem areas, the center belonged to the boys. A big L-shaped couch with a spacious square coffee table and a giant TV were in the middle of the room, and the boys had made this zone their nest. School papers, art supplies, TV and game console remotes, and board games spilled everywhere. Al-though Deena was fine with the boys doing their homework and generally camping out on the couch, we decided that at the end of the night the boys would have to pack up their backpacks and take them back to their room. We repurposed a basket (that had originally been on the bookcase full of junk) to hold the remotes, and we cleared all but a few useful school supplies out of the drawer in the coffee table. We left the games they played as a family—backgammon, Scrabble, and chess—on the shelf under the coffee table, and moved the rest of her sons' board games into their room.

The end result was an amazing change. Was Deena's living room ready for *Elle Decor*? Heck, no. She still had two middle-school-age boys and more than a full-time job. But her living room was now organized enough that she could find what she needed and not be embarrassed if she or her sons wanted to invite friends over on the spur of the moment. Moreover, she'd established a neutral setting, a resting point for her living area where everything was basically in its place, and knowing what this looked like made it easier to keep it that way.

Going forward, Deena and her sons each had to work to build a new habit: for Deena, working at her desk, and for the boys, taking their book bags back to their rooms at bedtime. Still, we had done such a major revamp that even with occasional backsliding, Deena felt a significant shift in her space and new confidence in her ability to stay on top of it.

The Organized Enough Living Room

- Have a designated spot for remotes.
- Practice a last sweep before bedtime so that things that don't belong go back to their proper rooms.
- Rather than adding more picture frames, replace outdated family pictures with new ones.

Fresh Eyes on the Craft Storage

Recently I met with a new client, Maggie. Though her apartment was spacious for one person, her quilting hobby had crept into every corner and was threatening to overwhelm the whole apartment. Maggie had quilting supplies in various plastic boxes and bins, but she couldn't find room to store them in one cohesive place.

Maggie had been looking at her space but not *seeing* it. Her apartment had evolved since she moved in. When she bought it, she had been working full time at a job that kept her extremely busy and traveling frequently. After she retired, she dabbled in several creative hobbies, from needlepoint to jewelry making, and then she got hooked on quilting. Maggie had an amazing amount of textiles and hoops and patterns, but she also had a fair amount of closet space, including one sizeable closet that she had devoted to quilting, which she told me was stuffed.

When I looked at that closet, I quickly saw that that a minor renovation would net her much more usable space. On the right-hand side were shelves of fabric—well organized but at maximum capacity. But the entire left-hand side of the closet was set up for hanging clothes, and although she had a few pieces of fabric on hangers, that side was mostly empty. Meanwhile, the floor was piled high with half-done projects in large plastic storage bags.

I've heard it said that clutter is "deferred decision making." I'm not sure that that is true of *all* clutter, but it certainly applied in the case of those bags. Maggie hadn't really been seeing the bags when she looked in the closet. When we took them out, it was time for Maggie to make some decisions.

As with all creative enterprises, Maggie had done some experimenting. Some of the bags held quilts she had started and then abandoned, others had particular patterns and cut fabric pieces ready to be used. For each, Maggie had to decide if she was really going to finish the quilt. Did she want to? Was it likely that she would? Could the fabric be stored with the other fabrics? Or was it better to just throw out smaller pieces and incomplete projects?

It's always hard to throw out work we have done and goals we have had. I have sat with people in their sixties who have trouble throwing out their college thesis. On the one hand, I get it: it's a part of you. On the other hand, I truly believe that when you let go of the old you make room for the new.

In the end, Maggie determined that most of those projects were lost causes; she had moved on to other quilts. I eliminated most of the bags and cleared the floor of the closet. We also sketched out a design to eliminate the hanging rod and expand the shelving in the closet so that it would be really functional as a storage space for the rest of her quilting materials.

Next, we looked around the apartment for more areas of stagnancy. We realized that there were just a few miscellaneous items stored in the built-in unit under her television. Clearing this area out took hardly any time at all. It was now the perfect place for the office supplies that had been randomly stored on several shelves in her hall closet. This in turn cleared a space for her sewing machine supplies, which was convenient, because the machine was located a few feet from the closet.

Having shaken the stagnancy out of her apartment, Maggie felt better. She walked several shopping carts of stuff across the street to the thrift store, and she gave a bag of quilting materials she no longer needed to members of her quilting community.

Maggie is typical of many of my clients in that she does know how to organize—her fabrics were beautifully arranged by color, and her templates had been gathered on one shelf— she just lacked perspective. Once she showed me what she had, together we began to see the possibilities. Maggie just needed fresh eyes to see where she could make a few key changes.

Organized Enough Craft and Hobby Storage

- Consolidate your craft items in one place. Resist the urge to squirrel away items in various nooks and crannies.
- Invest in accessible storage. If you can't get at it, you'll never use it.
- Whether it's balls of yarn or supplies for scrapbooks, be honest about how much you really need. Better to have less and use it more.

Bringing Fresh Eyes to Your Space

So how can you bring fresh eyes to your home? Here is my challenge to you: walk through your house as though you have never seen it before. What is dusty? What is cluttered? What is haphazard? What do you hate? What makes no sense?

Learning to look with fresh eyes is a powerful tool, and one that just takes practice. Here are a few exercises and techniques you can try to help you see your space in a new light.

Seeing the Forest Exercise

Right now, wherever you are: Close your eyes. Take a deep breath. Take a moment to stretch, roll your shoulders, and shake it out. Now open your eyes *without focusing on anything*. Let your gaze rest on what is in front of you. Resist "looking," which tends to put your focus on small spots; instead, try "gazing," if you will. Taking this larger view, you may notice clutter that never looked like clutter to you before.

Randomly try this at different times of day in different locations in your house. See if you can't begin to "see" differently.

Mirror Exercise

Another trick to seeing your space differently is to look at it in a mirror. For some reason seeing it in reverse helps us see it anew and makes us notice things that we had grown blind to.

Camera Exercise

Stand against the wall and just hold your camera up to take a photo of your room. Don't look through the viewer first. This is the opposite of getting a good picture from a good angle; this is the mug shot of interior photography. Again, sometimes the picture reveals things that you just haven't been noticing.

Artful Clutter

When I was a little girl, my mother used to take us to the ballet. We sat in the cheap seats (which weren't that cheap) but my mother told us that sitting high up in the ballet allowed you to enjoy the choreography better, as you could see the patterns that the dancers made on the stage. Still, my mother always brought the binoculars with which to enjoy the tiny, precise footwork of the ballerinas and the intimacy of the pas de deux. I always found it interesting to go back and forth between seeing the whole picture and then zeroing in on the perfect pirouette.

The ability to focus on the minute and also pull back to see the big picture is an important skill in organizing. You want to see your home like a director: make sure to view it from the cheap seats and from the focused spotlight. I love to artfully arrange what is left after the purge—what a meaner organizer might call clutter but I know is the stuff you love: the shell from Mexico and the rock from Maine can create a personal tableau next to your pencil jar, once you get rid of the stack of coupons that were wedged in between the rock and the pencil jar. Practice pulling your vision back and then zeroing in. You'll see your space differently, and that will help you know where to focus your efforts.

The Deadline Method

Are you a procrastinator? Do you work better on a deadline? Do you perform best in a crisis? For many people with clutter and organizing problems, having company over is a crisis.

Our homes should be warm and welcoming; to me, it's so much better to have friends over to share a meal than to go to a restaurant where it's noisy and expensive and they rush you out after two hours. It is awful, however, when your house is a disaster and all of a sudden your picky Aunt

Ruthie informs you that she is flying in for the holidays. So I say, don't wait for the crisis—control it.

Here is what you do: Set a date, and invite someone over to dinner. Don't wait for your place to be perfect. Do it now. Don't invite the really intimidating woman who just moved in down the road, but don't invite your BFF who has seen your home at its worst. Invite someone that you want to impress *a little bit*. It doesn't have to be a five-star dinner. Your home doesn't have to be perfect; it can just be *organized enough*. Sometimes all the carrots in the world aren't as effective as one stick. So plan that dinner party, create your own deadline, and get some energy around your home. I guarantee that as you spruce up before your guest arrives, you'll be seeing your place with fresh eyes.

Remember . . .

Practice new ways of seeing (mirror trick, camera trick, etc.)

Imagine that you are walking into your space for the first time. Notice what you see.

Cultivate your awareness of what's stagnant, gathering dust, or random in your home.

CHAPTER 4

Fear Creates Clutter

Thinking will not overcome fear but action will.
—W. CLEMENT STONE

Do you have a hard time letting go of possessions? Are certain areas of your home "stuck"? Are you overwhelmed by old clothing you can't bear to part with? Do you frequently feel guilty or anxious about throwing documents away? Facing your fears will enable you to FLOW.

I once had an acting teacher who told us, "Anytime you need to play an unsympathetic character, look for the fear. Negative behaviors usually boil down to some kind of fear." She was right, and it is no different with piles of clutter. Time and again, when I try to help clients figure out what exactly is causing them to save or hoard or hang onto a certain category of stuff, we come to a fear.

You could easily imagine a person who stockpiles canned food in case of a disaster, but the manifestations of fear are rarely that obvious. Fear comes in many flavors, and even the most successful and confident people can have irrational worries that cause them to cling to things.

Fear of Waste

I frequently see people hanging on to something that they no longer want or need because giving it away or throwing it out would be "wasteful." They think it has some monetary value, but they can't quite get it together to actually sell the thing. The truth is that usually it isn't really worth their time. Whether it is a dining table or a set of china, they might be able to sell it, but they would have to make and post an ad, ship the item, and so forth, and the net gain might be relatively small. Sometimes it's easier to just give it to a charity and take a deduction on your income taxes.

A weird thing has happened with the rise of Internet commerce. Antiques have become easier to find. Everyone is putting stuff from their attic on eBay, and as a result prices are coming down. Moreover, resale of home goods is highly subject to fashion; therefore, the expensive oriental carpet you bought ten years ago for thousands of dollars may be worth less than what you paid, because this year everyone is going modern. This leads into a subject we'll explore in the next chapter: know yourself. If you can't bear to give away something you spent a lot of money on, then you probably shouldn't buy something new until you have fully explored the likelihood of selling the old one. On the contrary, you may say, "No, what is important to me is that the room look really cohesive, and if I take a loss on the rug, so be it. I got ten good years of wear out of it, and that is good enough."

Don't be afraid to *let stuff go*. Giving away something you no longer want that might be worth a hundred dollars doesn't make you profligate, it makes you generous. Of course, if you have the time and energy to sell stuff, by all means, go for it. But if you don't, avoid getting stuck in the mentality that giving something of value away is irresponsible. Reclaiming your space is also valuable.

Financial Fear

In a related fear, many people get anxious when it comes to dealing with their finances. Whether caused by debt, uncertainty about the future, or just being unsure about the rules, the anxiety around our finances can be so uncomfortable that we avoid the subject at any cost, which of course becomes a self-fulfilling prophecy.

I see a lot of people who actually have a substantial amount of money, but they don't really understand it; maybe they grew up having less and were never taught about 401(k)s or capital gains taxes, or maybe they grew up wealthy and their parents didn't discuss it. Either way, feeling unsure of what you are supposed to do with money can cause anxiety that is reflected in your home. The result is often an instinct to hold onto stuff—every mutual-fund report (garbage!) or old, decrepit piece of clothing.

Most of my clients are relatively affluent, but when it comes to letting go of stuff, they get scared. It's as though holding on to an old duvet could save them if they lost their job. When my client Kristi was moving into a beautiful townhouse, she was reluctant to let go of an old alarm clock.

"Do you use it?" I asked her.

"No, I have a new one that's much better."

"So why not throw it out or put it in the donation bag?"

"What if the new one breaks?"

"Well, you will replace it."

"But what if I am out of work then?"

In the grand scheme of things to worry about, her mortgage and renovation costs would be a much bigger issue if she lost her job, which was not really likely anyway, because she was well respected in her industry. It was almost as though her anxiety had attached itself to little stuff like old alarm clocks so that she didn't have to face the anxiety caused by the much larger commitment of her mortgage.

When my twins were born, my own financial anxiety was so great that I accepted all the hand-me-downs I was offered. But the deluge required way too much sorting and took up too much space. I wish I hadn't been so fearful: the twins didn't need so many clothes, and sorting and storing made a lot of extra work. In retrospect, I could have said, "No, thank you," after the first bag and saved time and space.

Now I can't promise to pay your kid's college tuition, but if you truly grasp the principles of this book, you are going to spend less and waste less, and that is going to help you alleviate your debt and get a better handle on your finances. When we take a deep breath and hold our fears up to the light, we usually realize that there are simple steps we can take to lessen our anxiety. Whether it is calling our accountant or reciting, "My purse doesn't have to match my shoes, my purse doesn't have to match my shoes," once we identify our fear, we can vanquish it.

Fear of Litigation

Anxiety about getting rid of paperwork sometimes stems from a fear of litigation. "I need to keep this, just in case I need to prove it." Certainly there are times when this is necessary, whether it is proof of communication with a contractor or a payment to a hospital.

Coupons Don't Make the Cut

I'm just going to say it: I hate coupons. More often than not, they are clutter and an incitement to buy things you probably don't really need or you don't need two of. Sure, at first, they seem like a good deal. It seems wasteful to get rid of them. But coupons cause all kinds of anxiety for my clients: they keep them, stash them in random places, forget they have them, forget to use them, and then feel bad about it.

I urge you to resist keeping coupons, but if you do, have a system for using them. For example, if you get coupons for items you buy regularly, from a store where you shop frequently, keep them in your wallet. If you can get them digitally and keep them in your phone, that's even better.

If you stop keeping coupons, and you do what this book says, you'll end up buying so much less that you'll still spend less—even if you pay full price for everything you buy!

I have helped several people prepare for lawsuits in my career, and inevitably what is actually useful is buried in piles of paper that could have been disposed of years before. This makes the search much harder, more confusing, and frequently more expensive. The remedy is education. You need to know what you need to keep.

For example, in the case of a home renovation, you might be holding onto all kinds of papers:

- Records of payments to the contractor(s)
- Receipts for materials
- Scope of work documents
- Signed contracts

You don't need to keep bids from people you didn't hire, paint chips you didn't choose, or catalogs from hardware companies. You may, in fact, want to keep the paint chips that you did use—but in a file labeled *Decor* rather than with the legal and financial details of the job. People know a lot of this, but the task of sorting through stacks of papers becomes daunting, even more so when there is uncertainty. A great way to get a grip on your fears is to go into a sorting project armed with knowledge. Make step 1 a call to your accountant or a lawyer to find out what you really need to keep, and for how long, and then the sort will be focused and efficient, rather than painstaking and anxiety provoking.

Fear of Not Being Able to Find It Again

Many of my clients save things because they think they aren't going to be able to find that exact thing again. They save clippings of sofas they like and printouts from the Internet, and they make duplicates of important papers and file them in multiple places to ensure that they can find them when (if ever) they need them. Before you feel so smug because you do everything digitally, I have seen plenty of absolutely cluttered computer desktops, and I've heard lots of tales of computers crashing because there was so much stuff stored on them. Stop! The fear of not being able to find things is pernicious, because it causes you to save more things, which only makes it harder to find the things you need. Remember, *one is better than two.*

Have a little faith. If you really need it, you are going to be able to find it. I say, even if you think you might forget where you put a document and have to look for it in two places, if the places are orderly and not overstuffed, it shouldn't be a big deal. Instead of printing out an article from the Internet, create a folder and bookmark for it on your browser. Or simply trust that you'll be able to Google it again when the time comes. More than once, a client has clipped and then mislaid some article and I have succeeded in finding it online, only to discover that it was so old that the resources listed were out of business. Things can be simple. Not every decision needs to be a research project.

Fear of Needing It Again in the Future

What if they stop making them? What if the library doesn't have it? What if I can't find it online?

Or in the case of Doris, "What if I get a run?" Doris was a well-dressed client with hundreds of pairs of stockings. *Hundreds.* Sheer and opaque; nude, black, green, and gray. Knee-highs, control top, thigh-high. She had the perfect color and style of hosiery to compliment every item in her extensive wardrobe. Not only that, she had multiples. Gently, I tried to question her more closely about why she needed so many. "Well, sometimes I get a run. I like to have extra—just in case." "In case of what?" I asked. She couldn't quite answer. As I probed, I saw that even though Doris was in her seventies, and successful by every measure, getting dressed in a certain way was both performance and armor. The thought of going out in the wrong color hose caused her anxiety. This may seem silly to you or me, but most of us have something—and frequently, a collection of that something—we wouldn't dare go out in public without. Don't try to take away my lipstick.

In the end, Doris let me get rid of a lot of her hosiery. It turned out that much of it was so old that the elastic was shot. We weeded and winnowed, and I urged Doris to try to rethink her fashion choices: Instead of feeling like there had to be a particular color for every outfit, could she try to simplify and trust that nude or black would go with everything? By analyzing her need to be perfectly styled, Doris began to realize that it wasn't that important. When it was an undiscussed rule, alive only in her brain, it had the power to cause her anxiety, but once she could see it and name it, she could say, "So I have to wear the nude hose with the navy suit, I'll live."

Perfectionist's Fear

Perfectionism is often a big part of fear. Doris's fear was of not having enough, but it was also a perfectionist's fear. She wanted to know she had backup so she would always be perfectly dressed. "What if I need it?" "What if it's valuable?" "Aren't I supposed to make albums with all these photos?" In a way, all of these questions are about perfectionism. Underneath these busy, successful women (and perfectionism seems more pervasive among my female clients), I hear anxious, high-achieving little girls, who don't want to do it wrong. Maybe I hear it because I recognize it (I named my organizing business the Perfect Daughter, for heaven's sake) but I'm here to tell you that it's a trap. You'll never be perfect, just frustrated, and, really, is that how you want to live?

When I first met Christine, she was in her late thirties, but her apartment had the temporary look of a college dorm room even though she owned it and had lived there for nearly a decade. Christine's perfectionism had paralyzed her: she was afraid to buy a file cabinet for fear she would buy the wrong one, and she was afraid to paint because she might pick the wrong color. Slowly, she faced her fears, first buying a filing cabinet and, in time, redoing her entire apartment and even entering it in Apartment Therapy's small-spaces contest. Not only that, but on a professional level Christine went back to graduate school and found a career she loves and at which she is excelling.

I wish I could claim all the credit for Christine's success, but it wasn't overnight and it wasn't about me. Really, it was about Christine's growing ability to confront her perfectionism and walk further and further into uncomfortable places, both in her career and in her home. In the long run, her work situation is in a much better place, and her apartment is much, much more comfortable.

Procrastination, Perfectionism, Paralysis

There's a link between procrastination and perfectionism. In fact, many scholarly articles have been written on the matter. It reminds me of my sophomore year of college, when my best friend, Jeannie, was weeks late in handing in a big paper. The later the paper was, the more perfect she believed it had to be to justify its lateness. This, of course, was paralyzing, so she did nothing. It made *me* a wreck.

Done is good. Done on time is better. Perfect is a mirage. Forget perfection. Just do it—whatever it is.

Perfect or Not at All

Tammy was another client stymied by perfection. She was one of the worst hoarding cases I have ever worked with.

When I first entered her third-floor walk-up, she was in dire straits. She stood to lose thousands of dollars in medical reimbursements if she didn't file her claims by the end of the year, just a few short months away. At the same time the IRS was auditing her, and she needed to document deductions she had claimed for her business for the past several years.

Her place was a warren of knee-high stacks of newspapers and piles of unopened mail; magazines and catalogs covered each and every surface. Painstakingly we went through every pile, discarding, shredding, and filing. We collected the documents she needed and created orderly files for them. We literally had to work our way through shopping bags of paper blocking off the file cabinet.

When we were finally able to access the file cabinet, you can imagine my surprise when I opened the drawers and found they were perfect. Really, like a photo-shoot file cabinet: well organized, beautifully labeled, not too crowded. It was almost as if they were too good to use, which perhaps was why she hadn't touched them since the day she had set them up, years before.

Tammy made me see something that I hadn't fully realized: many seemingly disorganized people are actually frozen by their perfectionism. In contrast, my (highly functional) file cabinet is dog-eared and pretty full, and yet I can usually pull out exactly what I need in under thirty seconds and put away what needs filing just as quickly. When you use things—kitchens, clothes, file cabinets—they get worn. But that's okay. Remember *The Velveteen Rabbit*? I think unused stuff is sad. I have a purpose, you have a purpose. Let your stuff serve its purpose.

Tammy's late father, to whom she had been very close, was a lawyer. He had inculcated her with an old-school, document-saving mentality. The result was that she was afraid to throw out anything.

Ironically, it was her hoarding that left her so dysfunctional that she ended up having to scramble around looking for documents: Her tax audit might never have happened had she been more organized and filed a more accurate return in the first place. And if she had kept up with her insurance claims, getting reimbursed wouldn't have become a crisis.

FOMO: Fear of Missing Out

In *Reclaiming Conversation*, Sherry Turkle describes FOMO (fear of missing out): young people, not really engaged in the party they are at, checking their phones to see whether there is a better party down the street. This image really gets my inner hippie riled up: *be here now, man*. But FOMO isn't an affliction limited to millennials and their phones. It can strike anyone—the Upper East Side matron with a thousand invitations for every art opening and Broadway play in New York, the working mom with a sheaf of school flyers piling up on her desk, the successful real-estate executive with an endlessly growing pile of newspaper clippings—they can't throw stuff out because they think they need to attend every function and read every article. But no one can do it all.

Nor is it only events that people fear they are missing. It is knowledge, in the form of saved articles or digital bookmarks, it is their children's childhoods, it is the feeling of being relevant and "with it" as they get older.

But here's the thing: This holding on never makes it better. Hoarding invites and holding onto flyers for school events doesn't give you the time or energy to attend them. In reality, it sucks away time and energy as you sort and stack them. Keeping articles doesn't make you read them, and clipping, bookmarking, entering into Evernote. . . . These all take time. You have to be brave enough to say, "This I can do, and no more." Once you have said that and made a clear, authoritative executive decision, then you can really commit yourself to enjoying those events and articles that you *do* have time for. Think of the relief you'll feel that comes from letting go of 90 percent of the stuff that comes your way, so that you can really concentrate on the choicest 10 percent.

How Do You Let Go of Fear? Practice

Before you can alleviate stubborn clutter, think about what kind of fear may be driving it. Is it fear of waste? Financial fear? Fear of litigation? Fear of not being able to find something again? Fear that you are going to do something wrong (a.k.a. perfectionist's fear)? Fear of missing out? Identifying your fear will help you take steps to overcome it.

Walk through your space and really look at it with those "fresh eyes." What do you think is going to happen if you throw out Grandmother's yellowed linens or those bank statements from ten years ago? Ask yourself whether your fear is rational.

Can it be alleviated by education? Perhaps you are worried about getting rid of the linens because they may be valuable. Can you research what vintage linens are going for on eBay? If you are concerned about shredding old bank statements, can you ask your accountant whether the statements are still needed? Don't surrender to your fears—hold them up to the light and pick them apart. They may be flimsier than you think.

Remember that we are aiming only to be *organized enough* and that the first FLOW step, *forgiving ourselves*, is key. Once you know how to forgive yourself, the possibility of making a mistake is less traumatic. But it isn't a one-time event—it's a process. Most of all, it takes practice. Practicing letting stuff go and finding out that you are okay with it is a form of confronting your fear. As with any practice, it gets easier the more you do it.

Remember . . .

Identify the fear. Is it fear of lack? Fear of doing it wrong? Or another fear?

Hold the fear up to the light: Is it rational?

Alleviate the fear: do the research and talk to the experts.

CHAPTER 5

Who Are You Now? or, Will You Really Use That Bread Maker?

I know myself, but that is all . . .

—F. SCOTT FITZGERALD,
THIS SIDE OF PARADISE

Fitzgerald understood better than most the double-edged sword of the American dream. He also created the character of Gatsby, the iconic self-made man and yet a tragic one. Today, almost a century later, a vast world of products to buy makes it possible for the average person to reinvent herself anytime she likes. But it is a constant merry-go-round: If you can be anything, what should you be? How can you hope to know what you need if you don't know who you are?

Advertisers are canny: they spot our vulnerabilities, whether they are selling Dos Equis beer (who doesn't want to be the most interesting man in the world?) or Dior lipstick ("Shine, don't be shy"). In five minutes of paging through a catalog recently, I was sucked in by the following ad copy: "WHO'S THAT GIRL? She's LAID-BACK, but not scared to stand out. She's POLISHED, but not perfect. She knows that covering up is sometimes SEXIER than baring all. Her STYLE is her own." I wanna be that girl. Don't you? And maybe the zip-tote on the following page ($298) will help me get there.

So much of clutter is the stuff we've been hanging onto because we, at one point, had a certain vision of ourselves— one that isn't quite current or honest. It is project clutter, like the knitting that has been sitting in the same spot for years. The bread maker that's still buried in the back of the closet, gathering dust. The boxes bursting with memorabilia for scrapbooks yet to be made. But it is also in the bedroom: the three-step skincare regimen (you've yet to do step 1), the size-4 suit, the chunky necklace you forget to wear. Gretchen Rubin, author of *The Happiness Project,* brilliantly termed these items "aspirational clutter." One of the sharpest tools in the organizational arsenal is self-knowledge. Most of us have it—we just don't like to use it, because it isn't always pretty. Letting go, especially of ideas about ourselves, isn't easy. As you confront your space, it is good to remember these three mantras of letting go:

- The universe is abundant—letting go of the old makes room for the new.
- When I have time, something new will appear.
- I already have everything I need.

Trite? Maybe. True? Definitely. Do we forget it all the time even though we instinctively know it? Yes.

In this chapter, you'll meet several people who were hanging onto past selves in the form of clutter. There is Jana (who you met earlier, squirreling away tote bags), an elegant lady in her seventies who still fits into her clothes from the '70s. Her eclecticism is admirable but problematic from a clutter standpoint. There's also Aaron, a highly successful attorney, husband, and father whose penchant for buying luxury leisure equipment was quietly taking over all the space in his large (by New York City standards) apartment and frustrating his equally successful wife. Finally, I will share strategies for resisting aspirational buying in the first place as well as letting go of those pesky purchases from the past.

Who Do You Think You
Are When You Get Dressed?

Self-knowledge is particularly key in decluttering your wardrobe. Clothing presents one of the biggest letting-go obstacles for my clients. "That was then. Who are you *now*?" I ask them.

Bodies change, but life also changes. Just because you can still fit into your Versace minidress from 1999 doesn't mean you will be comfortable wearing it today. We view letting go of clothes as letting go of our past, and maybe on some level that is true, but it is also a good thing. You want your closet to be vibrant and full of fun stuff that you love to wear now, not a graveyard of past lives.

I used to be an actor. I absolutely believe in the power of costume and the importance of presentation—but I also know that you can get pretty far with a black turtleneck and a good story. Just as an actor has to be vigilant with himself to guard against false notes, we all have to be rigorously honest about who we are and what we genuinely like to wear.

Do we *want* to be the person who would wear a skintight leopard-print dress, or *are* we that person? Sometimes we buy clothes to try to become a certain kind of person. More than a few times, a client has told me, "Even though everyone at my office dresses very casually, I want to start dressing more professionally, because I think it will help me move ahead in my career." Excellent; I support that. But in actor-speak we would say, "Commit to that choice." From an organizing perspective, that means that you can keep those new suits you bought, but you need to donate several pairs of khakis and a bunch of the jersey tops that you used to wear to the office before you decided to scale up your wardrobe.

Jana, a well-dressed client, went through such a rigmarole to switch out her clothes every spring and fall that she often forgot where she had stored them. But it never really mattered anyway, because she had so many clothes that even if she lost a suitcase-full in the attic for a year or two, she still managed to be stylish all year long. Ultimately, Jana got tired of the stress of switching and storing and shuffling. When I first worked with her, our focus was on maximizing her closet space and creating systems. Right away I urged her to curb her shopping, because she already had so many clothes, and she tried, but it was a struggle for her. When she finally got sick of the effort she had to put into maintaining such a vast wardrobe, she was ready for a deeper self-assessment.

Jana, with my help, had to ask herself the tough question: "Who am I now?" Jana is blessed and cursed to have worn the same size for more than fifty years. She also has a great sense of style and is not a slave to fashion. She might pair new Prada trousers with a tweed blazer she bought at a thrift store twenty years ago, and it will look great. Jana's challenge was to decide who she is in her seventh decade. Once we really homed in what her current needs were, she began to see what she could let go of.

She often goes to the theater and opera, so some dresses could stay, and she travels a lot, so she kept garments that were easy to pack. But she no longer works in an office, so she didn't need as many blazers and suits as she had. And though she is as slim as she was fifty years ago, she had to admit she no longer liked the way her arms looked in sleeveless dresses. As much as I thought her arms looked fine, I was thrilled that she was eliminating twenty garments in one fell swoop! Jana also realized that just because she could still fit into her miniskirts and shorter dresses didn't mean she was wearing them—she didn't have the knees she had at thirty. Although tights are great with a tweed mini in November, Jana decided that there were certain summer dresses that were too short to be flattering.

Jana will never (and I love this about her) be worried about being "appropriate," but she does realize that certain things are too *jeune fille* (French for "young girl"). Some pastel florals just didn't suit her anymore, and although they held great memories, she had to release them. Similarly, she let go of colors that she liked but that she decided weren't good for her anymore. Acid green and yellow might have looked great when she was tan, but these days they were just making her look peaked, now that she follows her dermatologist's recommendation to stay out of the sun.

Jana still has a lot of clothes, and I haven't completely cured her of shopping, but her closet is more functional and more truly represents where she is in her life now. Reducing the amount of clothing has also made her seasonal switch much simpler, and she no longer forgets where she has wardrobe items stored. She is still iconoclastic—if anything, distilling her wardrobe has made her "more" Jana, not less.

The Organized Enough Clothing Closet

- Get rid of hangers and plastic from the dry cleaners immediately.
- Group items first by category (i.e., all shirts together). Then, within that category, hang items by color (typically light to dark). Finally, put categories in length order, so you might have shirts, pants, jackets, skirts, dresses. This consolidates your "tall" space, freeing up room so you could, for example, store tall boots or a laundry basket under your shirts.
- As you remove items to wear, always place the empty hanger to the far right (or left, if you prefer).

Who Do You Think You Are, Having a Midlife Crisis?

You may have noticed that many of the examples I have given have been of women, and it's true that 75 percent of my clients are women (though often they are just the representatives for the whole family). Here is the thing about men and clutter: Sometimes they really don't have much— perhaps just a box of miscellaneous wires dating back to the '90s or vinyl records they can't part with—but when men are cluttery, their clutter is *big*. As in it takes up tons of space. It isn't too many silk scarves or tubes of lipstick; it's water skis, electric guitars, gigantic speakers, and golf clubs. I hate to be stereotypical, and there are exceptions, but often this is true.

I think of my clients Aaron and Katie, a very successful two-career couple. They had a large apartment but felt like they had no closet space. When I first met Katie, she was expecting her second child and needed to create more room. As we went through the apartment, I began to see the issue. "Does he fish?" I would ask. "Well, not in a few years. He went with his Dad, and he'd like to go again." "Does he play guitar?" "He used to, back in college; he'd like to again." It turned out all the closets were filled with Aaron's gear of various long-forgotten hobbies: Fly-fishing, skiing, golf, guitar. In multiples. Top of the line.

Aaron was a good guy, and he had limits—I don't think he ever bought a sports car. But purchasing expensive equipment for hobbies he didn't have time for was a kind of magical thinking: "If I buy it, I'll do it." Sorry, Aaron, but it's just not true. Katie and I gathered it all up and put it in a storage locker. I imagine it sits there still.

What do those unused objects represent? Life is full of choices: We start a family, we are offered a huge job with a big paycheck, but maybe they don't leave us much time for our other interests. Embrace that. Wherever you are in your life right now, own it.

I deal with space for a living, and I can't help it if sometimes I read more into it than perhaps I should. When I saw all of Aaron's leisure equipment crowding out his wife and son, it seemed almost like he was subliminally digging in his heels: "I may have a wife and child, but I am still the cool guy who plays guitar. I may work seventy hours a week, but I am going to go fly-fishing one day." It is funny how when stuff just sits there it seemingly holds potential, but when you pull it out of the closet and try to justify it, the argument falls apart. You realize that you have used these skis twice and there are already newer, better ones that you could rent the next time you're on the mountain. And instead of a complicated fly-fishing rig, you might just want to buy two inexpensive fishing rods at Walmart so you can take your son fishing in the Hudson River. If you let those aspirational items gather dust, they just become a museum of your past ambitions, and that is kind of depressing.

If Aaron continues on his current career trajectory, I imagine he will be able to retire young and afford the latest and the greatest equipment when he does. In the meantime, he doesn't need to clutter up his closets with wishes. His life is good—he has an exciting job and a gorgeous family, and that is more than enough.

Who Are You?

Whatever area you are confronting—kitchen appliances, clothing, even papers—you can use this technique. Don't ask yourself, "Who have I been?"—that's for your photo album and memento box. And don't bother with, "Who do I aspire to be?" The only question that matters is, "Who am I *now*?"

When you go through your clothes, ask yourself what your intention was when you bought them. Ask yourself whether they are fulfilling that intention. Is the quantity appropriate? If you used to be home with your children and spent every morning on the playground, you might have needed a dozen T-shirts and a half-dozen pairs of jeans, but if you are now back at work and wearing business attire, you might wear jeans and tees only on weekends.

Spend time really analyzing what you wear in a week. Keeping a clothing journal for a week or two will help you stay honest about what you actually wear. If you go for weeks at a time without wearing a dress but dresses make up 70 percent of your wardrobe, perhaps you are not being truly honest about who you are, and you might not be allocating your space in the most logical way.

The same goes for stuff. Go through the kitchen: Do you make bread with the bread maker? Do you bake enough to warrant the variety of cake pans you own? Do you entertain enough to store as many serving platters as you have? The answer may be yes, or it may be that this is something that you really do want to do. In that case I say, Put it on the calendar. Make a baking date. Invite those friends over, because, otherwise, you are going to need to weed some of those platters.

Ask yourself:

Who am I now?

Do I use it?

Do I wear it?

Does it fit my current life?

Do I have too many?

"Someday" Clutter

What about project clutter: the knitting, the scrapbooks, the quilts, the photo albums? I am a creative person. I adore photo albums, I admire knitters, but I also know that we are all busy. Be tough with yourself when it comes to those things you'd like to get to someday. Ask the hard questions:

- How important is it to you?
- Are you ever going to do it?
- Can you schedule a date and time to do it?
- Is there a simpler way to do it?

Frequently I have advised clients to let go of the dream of albums and settle for photo-storage boxes by year (obviously, this is for all those old pictures, from before you went digital). I tell them that if they get all their photos into boxes sorted by year, then if they ever do want to make an album, the first step is done, but this will be *good enough* for now, and possibly for always.

Many of my clients are working mothers, and many have saved things to make a baby book for their child; meanwhile, that book hasn't even been started and SAT prep is well under way. Recently I was with a client who confessed to me that her college-age daughter had taken matters into her own hands and made her own baby book. There's nothing wrong with that! I say, *forgive yourself.* Let go of the book idea, which is labor intensive. Just get a box. Remember the endgame: you want to be able to show your children their ultrasound pictures, the bracelet they wore in the hospital, and the lock from their first haircut, but there is no law that it all has to be meticulously arranged in a book. A box can be just as fun for kids to look through. "You don't have to be Martha Stewart," I tell them. "And you don't have to be your own mother. Let the baby book go."

Then there is the big stuff that was useful at one time but no longer—the piano, the exercise bike, the nursery glider. Years ago you wanted to learn to play piano, so you paid to ship your Aunt Fannie's piano all the way from Boston, and there it sits, gathering dust. People have made worse mistakes.

Again, forgiving yourself is key. If the offending furniture has been there for five years and all it does is create friction with your spouse (who would like to put a desk in that space) then it is time to let go.

Is your exercise bike a valet, storing the clothes that can't fit in the closet? Step 1: make it usable. Step 2: give yourself a time limit. If you haven't used the bike for two weeks after you cleared it off, then, *adios,* Exerpeutic 900x.

At first, people get sad when I urge them to let go of these pieces. They feel they are dreams unfulfilled, and they are— but I remind them to focus on all the dreams they *are* currently fulfilling. They have a better job than they ever dreamed of, or they have twins, or they travel the world on a wonderful vacation each year. Sometimes I think we are too hard on ourselves. A little gratitude for what we *do* have can make letting go of that aspirational clutter a little bit easier to take.

Remember . . .

As you evaluate your items, don't ask who you were.

Don't ask who you aspire to be.

Ask yourself, Who am I *now*?

CHAPTER 6

Don't Let Paper
Push You Around

North Americans still consume more paper
per capita—upwards of 500 lbs. annually—
than anyone else on earth.

—FORESTETHICS.ORG

I've devoted a special chapter to how to approach paper, because this is the biggest hurdle for so many people. Paper is insidious, slipping into our homes a page at a time, until one day it's a completely overwhelming avalanche that has to be dealt with because there might be something important in that pile.

When I first entered Dorothy's home, I wondered why I was there. It was perfectly decorated, with every exquisitely chosen objet d'art in place. Then we went into the office, where the gorgeous white-lacquer desk was buried under a sea of paper. Paper was Dorothy's bête noire.

To me, it was obvious that the office was ground zero, but she avoided it. Over many organizing sessions, Dorothy focused on other projects that she deemed more important. Like many people, Dorothy is capable of intense focus—when she is interested. But she can be completely scattered when it is something she wants (subconsciously) to avoid. As we continued working together, I realized that we would often turn our attention to the office during the last hour of a session, which created a lot of unnecessary stress. I suggested that we spend the first hour, but only an hour, in the office. This lowered the stress, for both of us. Knowing it was a limited window of time allowed her to relax and focus, and working on it first thing enabled us to face those daunting piles of paper while we were still fresh.

As with many clients, I taught Dorothy the basics of paper management, like recycling as much as possible the minute it arrives, and how to sort the remaining mail into basic categories like bills, invitations, action items, and events. Though Dorothy may never enjoy dealing with paper, at least now she has systems that she knows work and she can use them.

In this chapter I will give you proven systems to manage all the different kinds of paper clutter. Last, because people now have digital clutter in addition to paper clutter, I'll show you how to create a mirror system for your digital files.

Decide What to Keep and Where to Keep It

The first thing we need to address when we discuss paper is what you need to keep. Some are obvious, like tax returns. But the fate of other documents seems murky, at first. Often when people feel overwhelmed by paper it's because they don't know, or think they don't know, what they should hold onto. Face it: if I gave you a two-foot-high pile of old Amex bills and told you to sort them by year and then arrange each year by month, you could knock out this task in an hour. But if I interspersed that pile with random receipts and medical forms and birthday cards, you would feel overwhelmed.

If you have a big backlog of old files, it might be worth a call to your accountant, or at least a few minutes spent researching online, to give yourself some guidelines. Then, you can create rules (i.e., I'm keeping all my tax returns, I'm throwing out everything else that's more than three years old, and I'm saving only year-end IRA statements). This way, sorting goes more quickly, and it's easier to delegate if you have someone to help you. You don't want to think too hard about each piece of paper; you want to be able to reduce the pile by 50 percent right off the bat.

In general, here are documents you do and don't need to save, and for how long:

Tax returns: Keep. Although some sources say three to six years, others say you should keep the return itself forever, particularly if you take a lot of deductions.

Tax backup: Three to seven years. The 1099s, the contribution receipts, and so on. Ordinarily you can pitch after three years; if you are very cautious, keep for up to seven.

Credit card receipts: One month (until credit card statement arrives) unless it is a tax deduction or what I call a major investment, that is, a bike, a watch, something you would want to file an insurance claim for if it was stolen or damaged.

Credit card statements: Generally I save these for the year, unless there are lots of tax deductions and that is a more accurate reflection than the receipts (for example, if you make charitable donations online using a credit card). Some clients just keep them with the tax backup and pitch them at the same time for simplicity's sake. It depends on your space and how likely you are to need them.

Bank statements: Keep for the same number of years as you keep your tax backup.

Brokerage/retirement statements: Most of this is easier to deal with online, and they are huge space suckers. It used to be that you saved your purchase date, but now it is all computerized. The only caveat is if you bought something pre-computers, or inherited stocks pre-computers, then if you actually have that purchase date, you can keep it. Other than that, you can keep for a year and then just keep the year-end statement with the tax backup and pitch when you pitch that stuff.

Medical, procedure related: Keep so that you have the information at your fingertips if you see a new doctor.

Medical/insurance, payment-related: Purge as you go or at the end of the year UNLESS there is dispute about a payment.

Keep, in general: Things that are PROOF: transcripts, diplomas, professional licenses, signed contracts, closing documents, inspection reports.

Of course, these are just general guidelines. Check with your accountant or financial adviser or lawyer on your own situation. Different states and different industries have different rules and regulations.

The second thing we need to address is where you are going to keep those papers you do need to hang onto. Traditionally, you keep papers in a filing cabinet. Binders can work in certain situations, such as projects that require you to take papers out to a meeting or back and forth from one location to another. File boxes are okay if you are really tight on space. But, honestly, most people, even in this day and age need at least one file cabinet. People have such resistance to filing cabinets, and I don't understand it. To me, a well-organized, oft-used filing cabinet is a beautiful thing. You can easily see what you have, access what you need, and everything works.

So here's my advice: Stop being in denial. If you have more than one pile or box or shopping bag full of paper, you need a file cabinet. A two-drawer will suffice for most people, but as always you should consolidate and weed to see how much you really have before you buy. If you are tight on space, a two-drawer unit can make a good side table or even night stand.

To me, the most user-friendly way to set up a filing cabinet is to have hanging files with categories, such as *Monthly, Banking, Credit, Insurance.* Then within those files you could have manila files with subsets, such as *Rent, Electric,* or *Cable* under *Monthly;* and *Citibank* and *Wells Fargo* under *Banking.* I put the monthly up front, because that is what I touch the most. Insurance can go farther back, because I only access that a few times a year. It is also helpful to put all the tabs of the hanging folders in a straight line. Counterintuitively, it is actually easier for you to read them in a straight line than zigging and zagging back and forth. It looks better too.

Why Are You Keeping it?
Where Is It Going?

Every piece of paper needs a resting place and an exit strategy. Your files are the resting place, but it is important to have an exit system.

When my new insurance policy arrives, I put it in the file, and then I stand the old one up so it sticks up and write SHRED AFTER JUNE 30 or whatever the date is that the new one kicks in. That way, the first time I open that drawer after June 30, I'll shred that document and get it out of the drawer.

With my taxes, it is a yearly process. At tax time I shred everything from the previous year that I don't need for taxes and I also shred my tax backup from seven years ago, thus making room for the new year's materials.

Anytime you make a file, you need to think about what the exit strategy is.

After all, you could probably live with only a two-drawer file cabinet forever if you are vigilant about getting stuff out of it on a regular basis.

Papers Need a Path

We'll talk more about systems in the next chapter, but it's important to get into some basic paper systems now. Remember when I said that your home is like an organism, with things coming in and going out? Everything that comes into your home, especially the paper, needs a path. And the path needs to be clear. Paper needs an entrance, a "port" where it gets handled, and then either an exit or a resting place.

Different homes have different systems, and I am going to tell you about mine, not because it's perfect, but because it is pretty simple and it has been working for close to twenty years.

1. My husband and I have side-by-side desks, which are really just countertops on file cabinets. When the mail comes, I sit at my desk and open it.
2. I shred a lot of it: credit card solicitations, bank advertising. I recycle the envelopes, the catalogs, the campaign flyers, and any other junk that arrives.
3. I put any bills to be paid on my husband's side of the desk under the paperweight, because he handles those in our household. The paperweight is his "in-box." He looks at the two or three things under his paperweight every night. If it is a bill, he has a file he keeps for that, and he pays those twice a month. I also might put the occasional auto-insurance renewal, which he can just glance at and return to me. I might also put something that has arrived in the mail for him, like an alumni magazine from his university, in his in-box. Those he would probably peruse over a few mornings and then put in recycling.
4. Then I take any invitations or other miscellaneous papers (there isn't much) and deal with them. An invite I might RSVP and put on the calendar, a seasonal schedule from a theater company I might put into my events folder, a rewards coupon from Staples I would put right into my wallet.
5. After my husband pays the bills, the bill receipts go back on my desk under my paperweight, which is

actually a flat-bottomed rock I found at the beach a million years ago. I file them in folders labeled by type of bill: *Amex, Cell Phone,* and so on. I save these until tax season, at which point everything is emptied and either filed with taxes or shredded. One of the advantages to this system, from my perspective, is that though my husband writes the checks, I file the bills, so I see them. I think it's important for adults sharing a household to be aware of all the finances.

6. Any other papers that come into our house also go under my rock. These include papers from my kids' school, insurance forms, camp forms, and so forth. My rock, as you can see, is my to-do/in-box, and I like that it is right there for me to see. It isn't always pretty, but the stack underneath is rarely more than an inch high.

Try to deal with stuff on your desk every day, even if only for a few minutes. Some days I don't have much time and I do little more than open the mail, but, because I sit down at my desk every single day, I don't really miss deadlines or forget about filling out forms. At night if I am tired, I tend to do easy tasks, like filing paid bills, putting school events in my calendar, and so forth. I save the harder jobs, like filling out camp forms and making phone calls, for the days that I work from home and am able to sit at my desk when it is quieter.

For people who work full time, establishing this can be hard, but you need to find a time, whether it is Saturday morning or Sunday afternoon or even super-early on a weekday morning. In the end, you save time by keeping on top of your game, and although it can feel unfair to have to do paperwork on a weekend, trust me, it is easier to do a little bit every weekend than wait for a crisis and have to spend the whole weekend digging out.

Another consideration is this: some people work full time and have offices. Often they keep some personal bills there for a variety of reasons: because there is more space, because they tend to pay bills while they are at work, and because bill-related phone calls have to be made during business hours. That is fine. But I encourage people to keep everything together, whether it is at work or at home. It is confusing to have the bills at work and the contract at home, or whatever the situation. Consolidating is key to organization.

Tax Returns

The other system that my husband and I have involves taxes. When we do our taxes, we pull all of the current year's bills out of their folders. We tally what is tax deductible, and we shred what needs shredding (anything with our address or account numbers; sometimes only the top half of the page or the first page warrants shredding). The folders are now empty and ready for a new year of bills, no new labels required.

In our household, we keep hard copies of all our tax returns and save seven years' worth of tax backup documents in clear, plastic envelopes. (Ask your accountant how long you should keep your supporting documents—not everyone needs to keep seven years' back.) At tax time, we pull out the plastic envelope with our taxes from seven years ago and shred all of the backup material, keeping only the returns. I then relabel the plastic envelope and fill it with the documents for the most recent year. I then push everything back in the drawer and put the newest year in front. I used to fear that one day I would run out of space in my file cabinet for taxes, but as more and more becomes digital, my paper backup gets smaller and smaller.

You might be saying, "So old-fashioned! Why doesn't she pay her bills / do her taxes online?" I think paying bills online and eliminating paperwork is ideal, actually! If you can do these tasks online, so much the better. But, for our household, because this is the system we have and it has been working, we haven't bothered to change it. Remember: *organized enough*—not perfect. But know that a digital file system can work almost identically: my business is largely online, and I create the same categories of files for my on-line receipts as I do for my paper receipts. The system is the same: a file per year divided by categories, but for the digital files I simply delete rather than shred after a few years. We'll look at creating a digital mirror system shortly.

The most important thing to remember is that every piece of paper or digital document has a path, and for almost everything, that path eventually leads out the door, whether the door is actual or virtual.

Medical Files

Seth was a computer engineer who freelanced, going from one big project to another. Because he worked for himself, he had his own health insurance and frequently changed policies to get the best deals. Seth had had a number of surgeries and medical issues over the years, and his medical files were a disaster.

After some discussion, I advised a separation that works for several of my clients: place medical insurance (read *money*)–

related documents in one file, and doctor/medical (read *health history*)–related papers go in another file.

This works because the insurance documents are pending: once the claim is covered, you can throw it out. In Seth's case, he saved the insurance paperwork until tax season because he thought that if he had another surgery and subsequently missed a lot of work, his medical expenses might actually hit 10 percent of his gross income, which enables you to deduct them from your taxes. At tax time, he could use the documents to tally up the total and keep it with that year's taxes, or pitch them if he wasn't going to deduct it.

As for his medical records, Seth decided these would be placed in a permanent file. Seth wanted to keep track of the various medications and procedures he'd had over the years, so that if he went to a new doctor he would have that information at his fingertips. Depending on how healthy you are and how computerized your medical practice is, and whether you trust them, you may not really need to keep much, if anything, in this category.

By creating this simple system, we were able to purge years' worth of moot insurance files and give Seth a simple template to determine whether he needed to keep something, for how long, and where to put it.

Your Active Files

Files in your drawers are for stuff that is done, or at least done for a while. They are for medical records and insurance policies and stuff that just sits there "in case." The top of your desk (or the easiest-to-access file in the drawer, if you prefer) is for active stuff, stuff that you are in and out of all the time. It's easier to get to if you categorize it—and neater looking—than it would be if you just left it all in a big pile. Access is one of the most important concepts in organizing. What good does it do to keep stuff if you can't lay your hands on it when you need it?

For me, and for many of my clients, a few desktop files are useful. Desktop categories are usually *Bills to Pay, To Do,* and *Events/Invitations.*

Bills to Pay is obvious, and another one to try to get online as much as possible, but still, sometimes you will get a paper bill. Some people like to pay them as they come in, but it is perfectly acceptable—and probably even time saving—to just sit down twice a month to take care of them, as long as you are consistent about it.

I like to have a *To Do* pile on top of my desk because I feel like if I file it away, I won't do it, but some people really hate even a small stack of paper on their desk. For them, I make a *To Do* file. If that's more your style, I recommend making a habit of looking through that file on a daily (or nightly) basis; otherwise, you are apt to forget what's in it.

Events/Invitations is an important category—some people even divide it into two separate files—because certain categories of paper still need a place in our homes. For example, certain special invitations, such as for weddings, still come in paper form, along with lovingly designed and carefully coordinated supplemental information on location, travel details, and so on. Although you should enter the time and date into your computer calendar, it's handy and less time consuming to keep the paper rather than enter all the other details.

Likewise, people receive lists and even catalogs of events (ask for the digital version!) happening at their favorite theater, local Y, or museum. Because you aren't going to go to *all* the events, but certainly you aren't going to sit down and make executive decisions about your social life for the next six months, you might simply want to hold onto it. Put it in the *Events* file on your desk, and when you're looking for something to do on a Sunday afternoon, there it will be.

Cutting Down on Visual Clutter

Dorothy, like many of my clients, is a very visual person. The highly visual have a conundrum: they hate to look at "active" papers on their desk, but they fear that if something gets tucked into a drawer, they will never deal with it. Dorothy definitely fell on the side of wanting to put it away; however, she compromised and put current projects into large clear-plastic envelopes, which she then labeled and kept on top of her desk.

Ask yourself what kind of a person you are. Do you need all of your folders to be the same color to cut down on visual clutter? Or do you like to have different-colored folders because a visual cue ("Oh yeah, *Events* are in the red one") will help you to grab the right file more quickly? Although I am generally opposed to plugging products or buying "cute organizing things," there are a lot of pretty file folders out there. I keep it basic manila in my file drawers, but on my desktop I have some fun and fancy folders, and because they are all different it helps me to easily grab the one I want when I need it. You can also find desktop vertical files. These are great if you are storing a few files on your desk, because a couple vertical files in the back will stick up and be easier to see.

I know, I know: It would look better if there was no paper at all on our desks, if it was all in the file cabinet and in matching, white folders. But we still seem to have paper, even in our online society, so try to stem the flow and organize what is left. And, remember, every filing system that works for your paper can easily be mirrored on your computer as you become more digital.

Organized Enough Papers

- Have a designated area where you deal with paper.
- Have a recycling bin and shredder in that area.
- Have a file cabinet or at least a box or tote for storage.
- Keep most-used files in the front of the easiest-access cabinet.
- Create categories for your hanging files, for example, *Monthly*, then within that *Mortgage, Maintenance, Cell Phone*, and the like. Farther back in the drawer I have a hanging folder, *Insurance*, and within that *Auto, Homeowners, Umbrella*.
- File by category, rather than year (e.g., *Tax: Contributions*) so that the files can stay year to year as you empty them out. Then, either shred or store with taxes.
- Make a point of discarding something anytime you pull out a file. It won't always be possible, but get in the mind-set of always looking for the opportunity.
- When your file cabinet is full, look to weed rather than buy another file cabinet.

Paper: Stemming the Tide

The simplest way to organize is to have less, and so it follows that the best way to reduce paper clutter is to have less paper. But how? What can you do so that less paper comes into your house in the first place? Ask yourself how each piece of paper arrived. Once you figure that out, you can make "stemming the tide" part of your routine.

When I first work with a client, I like to ask them where stuff came from: "How did this piece of paper land on your desk (or coffee table, or vanity, or bookcase)?" "Did it come out of your kid's book bag?" "Does the school offer an online notification option?" Just as I want every piece of paper to have a path once it is in your house, every piece of paper came from somewhere, and you can decide whether you need it and whether there is a way to eliminate it.

If your piles are made up of bills and bank statements, consider switching to online options. Investing twenty minutes to call or go online to switch could save you hours in opening, filing, shredding, and discarding. If you're constantly receiving requests for charitable donations, you can remove yourself from mailing lists that you don't wish to give to, and then you can ask charities you do donate to if they will contact you only via e-mail.

If your trouble is catalogs, remove your name from mailing lists. Always at the bottom of my to-do pile are back pages from catalogs that I am saving so that someday, when I feel like procrastinating for ten minutes, or I am waiting for the water to boil, I can make a few calls and get my name removed from some mailing lists. Though I have done it over and over, it seems they constantly crop up. I shop at a new store, and suddenly I'm on five new mailing lists. (Another reason to never shop.) You can also use Catalog Control and various online services to remove yourself from a bunch of mailing lists in one shot.

If you seem to have endless magazines and newspapers, you are probably subscribing to too many. Be honest about how much you can really read in a week, and then be ruthless about holding yourself to that standard. Let some subscriptions lapse, and see whether some of those you are keeping are available online.

Train yourself to take notes in your phone if you can. Despite the ubiquity of the smartphone, people still seem to collect scraps of paper, notes, and business cards. If you still end up with scraps of paper that you want to keep, either file them where relevant (say, notes from a conversation with your financial adviser) or tape them into a single notebook that you keep on your desk. This method is good for things you want to follow up on or add to your to-do list.

For business cards of important contacts, like a new doctor, enter the information into your phone's digital address book immediately, and toss the card. If it is a card of someone you might want to reach out to in the future, just have a place, even an envelope, where you keep all those cards together, so when you look for it, you can find it.

A Digital "Mirror System" for Files

"Never use two steps when one will do." This was what I needed to convey to my client Mary Anne when we started working together. Because Mary Anne was old school and a perfectionist, she tended to print things off the Internet to have a hard copy. For example, she donated to quite a few charities, and increasingly she gave online, so her instinct was to print out the receipt and file it (alphabetically) with the other receipts that she had received in the mail. Of course, I wanted her not to create more paper. I pointed out to her, as I have to many of my clients, that more and more of our records are going to be online and that the thing to do is simply create a mirror system on our computers.

A mirror system is just what it sounds like. In your file drawer you might have a file called *Taxes*. If I made it, it would be a hanging file and in it there would be subcategories, such as *Contributions, Estimated, Business Deductions,* and so on. I recommend that you do the same on your computer. Create a file for taxes and within that, by year, have subfolders with the categories you need. The reason you put the year on the digital and not the paper file is that the paper file gets emptied out at the end of the year and refiled with the next actual tax return. However, on the digital file you want to make it easy for yourself to be able to delete the whole file when it is time, without opening individual documents.

For example, Mary Anne gave to Meals on Wheels every month. She had set it up as an automatic deduction on her credit card (good job, Mary Anne!), and Meals on Wheels would send Mary Anne a monthly electronic notice after they charged her card. In the past Mary Anne had printed these out (step 1), filed them in her file cabinet under *Contributions* (step 2), and then totaled them up at tax time (step 3). In fact, she also entered them into her Quicken account, which would actually make it four steps, but we aren't even going to get into that! I suggested that Mary Anne create a file in her e-mail to keep the notices from Meals on Wheels, so that she would have them all together at tax time. I recommended making the files exactly like the ones she had in her drawer: *Tax 2014* and, within that file, another file called *Contributions* and one called *Office Supplies,* so that when she ordered online from Staples she didn't need to print that out.

It seems to me we are all tired, and I want to make getting organized as seamless as possible, so when I create a mirror system for a client, it is literally that, it mirrors the system they already know, so they don't really have to learn anything new. All they have to do is swap the habit of printing for the habit of filing on the computer.

Going Paperless

Everyone wants to go digital, and that's great if you are truly ready (though you still need to create a digital filing system), but when people want to scan piles of paper I get dubious. Scanning is often just an extra step. If you have a document in paper form and you truly need to keep it, it may be simpler to put it in a folder than to go to the effort to scan it.

Keep in mind that every piece of paper should have an exit strategy and that we are always weeding. So if you are keeping a doctor's bill until you are sure the insurance has paid it, you can just file it into a *Medical Bills* folder, and at the end of the year or when the drawer starts getting crowded, you can whip through that file in ten minutes and pitch everything that has been reimbursed. Getting to that point on the computer can be a long slog of opening and deleting documents. Yes, it's sometimes quicker to search and find a document on the computer (if you have labeled it appropriately), but when it comes to deleting files, having to open each document can be slower than glancing at a piece of paper. Most paper doesn't need to be kept forever, so keeping that system flowing (with paper coming in and going out) seems simplest.

I also find scanning to be a delaying tactic. You know you should throw out that old, insignificant letter, that mediocre picture your child drew, the closet plans from the company you didn't use. I suppose that a scan is better than a piece of paper, but really I am a rip-off-the-Band-Aid kind of girl. Why delay the inevitable? If you don't need it, you don't need it. *Let it go.*

However, if your financial institutions offer a paperless statement option, I encourage you to take advantage of it. It's great to go paperless for IRA accounts and other brokerage statements that take up so much space in paper form and are so much easier to deal with online anyway. Any bills, such as for credit cards or utilities, that you can access and pay online are great as well. You don't have to worry about storing digital files or paper; the institution stores it and you can simply access what you need. However, be aware that not all companies store the records in perpetuity, so make sure that if something has tax ramifications, you will be able to access statements for as long as you would have held onto the paper statement, whether that is one year or ten.

Whether you are old school or high tech, the same principles apply. Every paper or document needs a path, and knowing what you need to keep and for how long is key to keeping an orderly file system.

Remember . . .

Every paper needs a path—what comes in must go out.

The less paper you bring in, the less you have to manage.

Almost everyone needs a filing cabinet.

Digital files need to be organized, too.

CHAPTER 7

Better Systems =
Less Thinking

Wash on Monday,
Iron on Tuesday,
Mend on Wednesday,
Churn on Thursday,
Clean on Friday,
Bake on Saturday,
Rest on Sunday.

—LAURA INGALLS WILDER,
LITTLE HOUSE IN THE BIG WOODS

I introduce this organizing concept last, because it leads us
naturally into the next section of the book, habits. When
I say better systems = less thinking, I am talking about consciously creating a home for items and a routine around putting them away, so that upkeep becomes automatic.

So much chaos and clutter is a result of not having a good
place to put things. Hundreds of times I have asked clients,
"Is there a place for this?" and received the answers "Not really," "Sort of," or "Yes, but it's hard to get to." The goal is to
be able to do a lot of our maintenance without much effort,

because at the end of a busy day when we need to sort mail and put laundry away, there isn't too much brainpower left for grand decisions about where things belong.

A system is a dedicated method for how you do things and where items belong, which your habits will then support. When creating a system, whether we are setting up drawers for our clothing or our kitchen, it does require some thought initially. We need to be conscious about it. It doesn't matter if it's a regular spot for dish towels: if we take the time to be mindful about our system when we set it up, maintenance requires little to no thinking, and automatic is exactly what we are going for when we are building new habits. Putting in a little effort on the front end means that you can then coast along being organized enough.

What makes a great system? Two things: simplicity and consistency.

Simplicity is key. I hate unnecessary multistep systems and overly complicated processes. I like the shortest distance between two points. To make a good system, start by thinking about your goal: What are you trying to accomplish here? Organizing, at its core, is about being able to store what you have in a way that you can easily access it. Our ancestors didn't have this issue; it's only in modern times, when we have the luxury of so much stuff, that we need to create systems to find what we need.

When I was little, my mother loved to tell us the story of how she'd been asked to leave the library when she was a girl because she was laughing so hard at *Cheaper by the Dozen*, by Frank B. Gilbreth Jr. and Ernestine Gilbreth Carey. *Cheaper by the Dozen* is a hilarious memoir about growing up in a family with twelve children whose parents were experts at the forefront of the "efficiency movement." They tried to institute all kinds of time-saving efficiencies in their family, with some comic results. I think that because she read it at such an impressionable age and loved it so much, that book lodged in some deep part of my mother's brain and influenced her.

There is one efficiency that truly does save time: being consistent. Although it was totally annoying to me growing up that there was a "right" way to load the dishwasher, to fold my sweaters, and to hang my towel in the bathroom, in retrospect I admire that my mother had thought these things through. In my mother's world, putting all the silverware pointing down and all the plates in size order, was logical because it saved time on the unload. If you just dragged your towel over the rod, yes, it was off the floor, but it might not be dry by the next time you used it. If you smashed your sweaters into the drawer, then they ended up wrinkled. My mother believed that doing things properly could save time, make things work better, and make things last. I appreciate that she viewed housekeeping not as drudgery but as something that could be conquered by efficiency.

In the previous chapter, we created a system for dealing with the mail and paperwork. Now let's look at a few systems for other areas of your home.

A System for Clothing

If your goal is to be able to access the clothes you need and keep your drawers neat, you might approach it this way:

> Let stuff go. Get rid of excess clothing (outdated, doesn't fit, etc.).

Organize what's left. Group what is left into categories, like with like.

Give everything a home. And stick to those boundaries. Remember the goal: you need to be able to
easily find what you most frequently use:

Closet
   Dresses, suits, skirts, blazers, blouses (on the
      hanging rods)
   Shoes (on the floor or in shoe bags)
   Sweaters/fleeces (on the shelf above the hang-
      ing rod)

Dresser
   Top left drawer: bras and underwear
   Top right drawer: socks and stockings
   2nd drawer: T-shirts
   3rd drawer: jeans and casual pants
   4th drawer: workout clothes and sleepwear

Continue to weed excess items until everything fits in
your dresser and closet.

If there's a hard-to-reach area at the top of your closet,
you might put off-season or rarely worn clothes there and
put an alert in your calendar to remind you to bring them
down. But here's the rub: if anything starts to get overfull,
you have to weed. You can't buy new stuff and squish it in.
You have to let go of something before you bring in anything
new. Think of the closet and the dresser as boundaries (we'll
go into this more in Chapter 11, page 158), and now the system is to stay within them.

The Only Folding Rule You Need to Know

There is no single right way to fold, but, whichever way you choose, consistency is key in the folding department. *Make a conscious decision about how each type of item will be folded and stick with it.* You may want to experiment with the fold that fits best for the space you have. For example, in many drawers, jeans fit better folded into thirds. We fold my husband's undershirts into fourths, because that way they fit more neatly into his top drawer.

Better Systems, Not Perfect Systems

Emily's house was exquisitely decorated, but she confessed it sometimes took her days to put clean clothes away. When I saw her sock drawer, I immediately understood why. Emily's drawer system was overly perfect, involving baggies sorted by color and type: black trouser socks in one bag, sheer black hose in another, opaque black hose in yet another, and so forth. Too many, too complicated.

On the face of it, the drawer was organized. But getting it that way was much too labor intensive, and ironically Emily's system had made her clothes too hard to access. She had to rummage through multiple baggies just to find a pair of socks. I urged her to both weed—"Do you really need brown trouser sox?" "Do you need seven pairs of gray hose?"—and then to simplify. If she mostly wore black hose, maybe instead of having a bag for each other color she could have one other bag for any hose that weren't black. That way she could have four baggies rather than eight.

Sometimes it's actually more efficient to be organized enough than to be perfectly organized.

A System for Laundry

Once you've weeded your clothes down to what you really need and really love and you have a dedicated place for them, you will need to establish a routine of doing the laundry once a week.

A good laundry system takes place on the same day or days of the week. You might do clothes on Tuesday evenings and sheets and towels on Saturday mornings. There's no right way, but consistency is a must.

When you have a laundry system that works, you actually need fewer clothes. My kids need only three school uniforms because we do the wash on Wednesdays. There is no need for more than two sets of sheets per bed if you wash the sheets once a week. These things seem nitpicky and perhaps boring, but they are the scaffolding of a well-run life. If you have a washer and dryer at home, you may feel like you don't have to think about this as much, but it isn't much of a system—or very efficient—if you are constantly throwing a few pieces of laundry into the wash so that you can wear them the next day. You don't want to think about laundry because it is dull? Make a routine, and you won't have to think about it at all, you'll just do it.

A System for Housekeeping

My client Ginny, who was drowning in kids' stuff up in Riverdale, complained that somehow there was always a certain level of disorder to her family's home. Recently, I was with her when suddenly I grasped her problem. It wasn't the amount of space they had or the presence of little ones; it was how she saw housekeeping.

Ginny, like so many of us, was always busy. She was writing a novel, and she and her husband had a creative business that was taking off, not to mention her two rambunctious boys, the older of whom had just begun kindergarten. She knew she had to prioritize, and so she did. She put being a good mom at the top of the list by doing crafts with her kids in the afternoons, spending a lot of floor time building trains with them, and reading to them before bed most nights. She also tried hard not to neglect her writing, because like a lot of women of my generation she believes that it's important to maintain her identity outside of her children and because she wants her sons to see her both as a loving mom and as a professional person.

What fell to the very bottom of her (and her husband, Evan's) priority list was their home. In the evening, it felt more important to have reading time with the kids than to have a battle about putting things away, and in the morning there was always a rush to get everyone off to school and work.

Of course, Ginny and Evan weren't very happy with the state of their home as a result (which is why I was there in the first place). I saw clearly that the problem was that they had, without realizing it, devalued the very tasks that would make their home the comforting place they wanted it to be. They were always rushing but to where? There were little piles of things that hadn't quite made it back where they belonged. Their cabinets, although spacious and not overfull, had no plan. Their apartment was large but haphazardly arranged.

My clients are smart people. Some of them make a lot of money and many of them are in creative fields, but sometimes, in some deep part of them, they think that the ordinary task of putting things away is beneath them. They equate housekeeping with drudgery. But it doesn't have to be!

Sometimes it helps to spin something in your own mind. I advised Ginny and Evan to practice mindfulness with the mantra "household maintenance is not a waste of time." In fact, in his classic guide to meditation, the famous Buddhist monk Thich Nhat Hanh says, "I clean this teapot with the kind of attention I would have were I giving the baby Buddha or Jesus a bath." He spends much of the book talking about how any of the most ordinary tasks can give pleasure if they are done *mindfully*.

Ginny and Evan needed to learn how to find pleasure in their daily rounds. Life is full of seemingly boring tasks, but avoiding them makes them harder, not easier. Focusing fully on any task can make it more pleasurable and, get this, *more efficient*. It is paradoxical: by investing more time deciding where things go, you can actually spend less time putting them away. When Ginny and Evan didn't give any attention to creating a dedicated spot for the toys and the papers, their home became cluttered and unmanageable.

Ginny, Evan, and I spent several days rethinking and reworking their home. We tackled small issues, like how to fit a recycling bin into the already-tight kitchen and how to corral the art supplies in the dining room (because the dining table was also the homework/craft table) so they wouldn't look so messy but would still be easily accessible. We repurposed a small, stackable drawer unit that they already owned to be the art-supply cabinet. It lived on the windowsill day to day but easily stowed away in the boys' room when they had company over for dinner.

On my advice they decided to make putting toys away part of their bedtime routine with their sons. Sure, the boys might resist at first, but eventually not only would it make home a more peaceful place but they would be instilling good habits.

Likewise, Ginny could spend ten minutes straightening up before she started to write in the morning, instead of the usual thirty she spent fooling around on social media when she first sat down. Evan could clear up the kitchen while Ginny was helping the boys put away toys, so that when they sat down to watch television after the boys were in bed, the apartment would feel serene and orderly. Better yet, mornings would be simpler when everything was in its place.

We also spent time on both Ginny's and Evan's desks. Ginny had been working at the dining table and at her desk, and that scatteredness revealed itself in little piles of paper stuck here and there throughout the apartment. We talked about what papers came into the house and where they landed. Though Ginny and Evan had the bones of a system to deal with the paperwork from their business, they had never sat down and discussed a formal division of labor. Formalizing who does what can be awkward ("hey, I'm doing everything") but healthy for both couples and business partners, and especially for couples with businesses!

Here are the rules I gave Ginny and Evan: Every paper should have a path (see page 78), be it to the file folder or the shredder. Every item gets its spot on a shelf or a rack or in a basket. Treating objects with care will honor them, preserve them, and bring a sense of order and peace to their home. Just as the environmental movement encourages us to respect the earth and treat it kindly, I encourage you to treat your home and possessions kindly. Make housekeeping a creative act. Bring your whole self to it.

Where can you bring mindfulness to your home? Do you toss the outfit you decided not to wear over a chair? Make the effort to put it away so that it will be neat if you want to wear it next week. Which drawer is your albatross? Spend a few minutes weeding and refolding, and then practice mindfulness every time you open that drawer. Don't avoid the minutiae of housekeeping. Embrace it, lean into it, breathe through it. Housekeeping can be as Zen as you choose to make it.

Fewer Pieces = Better Systems

One problem that Ginny and her family faced was that of sheer abundance. They had too much stuff, much of it gifts from Grandma.

I urged them to bring mindfulness to this problem as well. One of the ways to shift our mind-set to consume less is to give more attention to what we have. Shoes shined? Clothes ironed? Thoughtfully getting yourself squared away is not beneath you. You need fewer things when you take better care of what you have.

We talked about thornier issues, like how to ask Grandma to buy less. Approaching people who love you and your children about gifts can be tricky, and sometimes it is an impossible hurdle. Still, some of my clients have had success with these methods:

- **Suggest something the child needs.** "You always give Junior so much, but our apartment is so tiny, and really, what he loves are those cotton pj's from Hanna Anderson. . . . They are so cute. Would you buy him a pair? I promise I'll send pictures!"

- **Suggest a special event.** "We are really trying to teach Sally that family is more important than stuff. Do you think that this year instead of gifts for her birthday you could take her to the Ice Capades/ botanical gardens/theater? I think it would be really special for her to spend some one-on-one time with you."

- **Suggest a membership.** "You are always so generous, but instead of more toys this year, what we would really love is a museum/zoo/aquarium membership for the family."

I know these strategies may not work on everyone, but it's worth thinking about what might work and what conversation you could have to try to minimize the influx of gifts.

Labels Keep Everyone on the Same Page

Labeling is one of those things that may seem like overkill, but can really be a worthy investment of time, particularly in homes with multiple people using a space or areas that are prone to clutter. Trust me, I'm not trying to make your house look like something out of a design magazine with charming hand-lettered labels tied to pretty baskets with dotted ribbon. Hardly! I just want your spouse to stop putting T-shirts in your son's jeans drawer, because everything fits if the T-shirts go into the right place. Labels are not about perfection; they're about clarity.

Karen and Paul are a successful New York couple with two small children. When I helped the family move into a new apartment, Karen and Paul were adamant that we needed to build in the organization from day one. Karen lamented that part of the chaos in her old place hadn't been caused by lack of space but by too many hands in the pot. With two parents, a nanny, a twice-a-month housecleaner, the occasional grandparent, and a three-year-old who wanted to "do it herself" all trying to help, keeping things in consistent spots was challenging. The move gave us the opportunity to start from scratch, put everything in a well-thought-out location, and then *label* it.

We labeled every shelf and drawer (if you put labels on the inner lip of the drawer, they won't show from the outside). We labeled her kids clothes: *Tees, Pj's, Pants,* and so forth. In the kitchen we did the same, putting labels on the shelves: *Sippy Cups, Mugs, Glassware,* and so forth. No one had to wonder where the Tupperware went or where to unload juice boxes after the Costco run. Everything was labeled, and everything fit.

When you are organizing any space, you are putting like things together, but people forget and people rush. If you have spent the time to put all your tea together on one shelf and all your pasta and grains on another and it is fitting nicely, then put labels on the edge of the shelves: *Tea, Pasta and Grains.* You can use a label maker, like I do, or you can use craft tape and a Sharpie, or mailing labels. The point isn't to be picture perfect but to remind everyone that there are "zones" so that they can find and also replace things easily. This will also help you with your inventory control: you'll know just where to look to see if you have enough flour

(*Baking*), and it will also remind you not to overdo it when you are shopping: "This pasta is on sale, but do I really need six boxes of penne? It won't fit in my pasta section, so I'd better not!" Labels are little reminders to keep everyone on track. You may think that it is too fussy or too time consuming, but really it takes ten minutes to label a kitchen after you've done the harder work of organizing, and it will help maintain that work so that you don't find yourself needing to redo it three weeks later.

Good Systems Change with Age

Finally, remember Joan, my client with decades of unsorted photos? Joan had a file system that was no longer working for her. For years she had perfectly good systems for filing her medical records. She was healthy, there weren't many, and what she needed she kept in one folder, which she periodically purged. As she aged, however, she had more doctors—and more papers, especially after she suffered a minor heart attack in her seventies. Her medical records were also complicated by the fact that she lived half the year in New York and half in Florida.

Ordinarily, I'm a big fan of the file cabinet, but Joan wanted to be able to take all the information back and forth from New York to Florida and she wanted to have it be very organized. We considered a few different systems before we found one that seemed right for her. Though I sometimes find binders to be overly labor intensive, they ended up being a perfect solution in this situation. We got Joan two 1-1/2-inch binders, one for New York doctors, one for Florida doctors. We put dividers with pockets labeled for each doctor and also plastic sheet protectors that she could use to stash prescriptions and other small pieces of paper. The binders fit into her carry-on when she traveled so she would always have her current information with her.

This system made it easier for her to find what she needed when, for example, her New York cardiologist wanted to see the results of a stress test her Florida doctor administered. It also made filing simple. Happily, Joan's husband dealt with the insurance in their family, so anything billing related we just passed on to him.

Joan's example is important, because no matter how good a system is, sometimes we evolve and outgrow it, and we need to develop a new one.

Better Systems Come from Practice, Not Genius

Sometimes clients say, "Oh my gosh, you are so good, how did you think of doing it that way?" But I'm not so smart; my brilliant insights, such as how to fold jeans into thirds to fit them into standard dresser drawers, aren't delivered in a blinding flash of light. As you move through your home and completely commit yourself to finding logical, accessible storage for all your belongings, instead of smashing them in or squirreling them away, you too will have flashes of inspiration. You will suddenly see that the spatula needs to go upside down in the kitchen drawer, and you will feel like a genius, and you are! Once you give attention and respect to what you previously thought of as mundane, you will begin to enjoy it. You will get better at seeing the solutions and the possibilities, and that will be very satisfying.

Remember . . .

Being mindful when you create systems will save time down the road.

Labeling can make maintaining the system easier.

Rhythm and routine make life run more smoothly.

Conclusion to Part I

> The future suddenly seemed as if it would be much more difficult than I had reckoned but it had also become much more real and more certain, instead of undefined possibilities I saw opening out before me a clearly marked field of activity.
>
> —SIMONE DE BEAUVOIR,
> *MEMOIRS OF A DUTIFUL DAUGHTER*

I hope that so far something you've read has surprised or even (and this would make my day) shocked you. I hope that you are seeing things in your home or office with a different gaze—with fresh eyes. If you are hearing my voice in your head when you start going off list at your local big-box store, then I've really succeeded. If you are thinking about your home as a living organism, if you are slowing down and being more mindful, if you are trying to bring fresh eyes to your space, then you are shifting your perspective. Maybe you are thinking about what fears trip you up, or maybe you are considering what parts of your self-image are at odds with your reality. Hopefully, you are more conscious of the paper and digital clutter coming into your space, and you are beginning to think in terms of systems.

Great! Now that we've shifted our perspective, now that our minds are open, now that we see the path, now the real work can begin. You have the concept; perhaps you see the pitfalls that have kept you on a hamster wheel of purging and organizing and cluttering for years or even decades. Now it is time for the secret sauce: creating habits. You are primed and ready. It won't be as hard as you think, and, in the long run, it's going to make all the difference.

PART II

Staying Organized in the Real World

Your net worth to the world is usually determined by what remains after your bad habits are subtracted from your good ones.
—BENJAMIN FRANKLIN

Part I of this book was about opening your mind so you could see your clutter and disorganization more clearly. Now that you have diagnosed your problem and found some solutions, it's time to take it to the next level—how to stay organized for good.

In the end, there is only one thing that keeps people organized. It isn't anything you can buy, nor is it a lightning flash of inspiration. In the end it's plain ol' boring habits. Just like your mother told you. As annoying as it is that our mothers were right about almost everything (I said, *almost*), it's comforting, too. It means that this isn't beyond us; it's just going take a little, ya know, *work*. But before you throw this book down and declare it is too hard, let me tell you this: if you develop these habits, life will get easier, because you are already working: searching and squeezing and shopping.

I'm just going to teach you how to focus your energies most strategically, so you can have the home you desire.

At some point in your life, you probably had someone tell you to develop a better habit. Whether it was a teacher, a coach, a religious leader, a doctor, or your mother, they were passing on knowledge they had received, probably from their mother, teacher, coach, whatever. Now, however, we have science backing up the wisdom of the ages.

In *The Power of Habit*, Charles Duhigg discusses the current scientific understanding of habit formation. He explains that by experimenting with a very simple formula (cue, routine, reward), we can use it to great effect. Habits are a neurological shortcut that develops in our basal ganglia, the very deep, primitive part of our brain. When we first learn something new, it is hard work and there is a lot of brain activity. But, as we stick with a habit, it requires less and less of our concentration, and brain scans reveal less and less activity. The coolest part? Brain scans also reveal that, once these habits are established, it is the basal ganglia that takes over. The basal ganglia provides us a way of conserving our mental energy so we don't have to think too hard about things we do all the time. However, there is danger in that—how do you make sure that you don't get sloppy (for example, leaving your keys in the door lock every time you come home)? You have a cue: you see a hook to hang the keys on or a dish on the hall table to drop them in, before you turn back and lock the door (your habit). A cue triggers a habit, which leads to reward. In this case your reward is knowing that you are safe and you always know where your keys are. That is your habit loop. Habits live in the substrata of our brain, where we don't have to think too hard; we just do. The reward triggers dopamine, which reinforces the habit by making us feel good.

For many of my clients, the majority of their organization problems stem from bad habits they aren't even aware they have. The habits that lead to clutter are often insidious but may seem benign: the mail somehow lands on the kitchen counter and never moves, people go to Costco for diapers and end up buying a whole lot of other stuff.

Our task now is to break down the disorganization habit, find the cue, change your habit loop, and focus on the reward: less waste, less clutter, and a more serene home.

Make Organizing Effortless

Decision making is tiring, and, after we spend all day at work making decisions, later that evening we are more susceptible to suggestion and letting things slide. In their book *Willpower: Rediscovering the Greatest Human Strength*, psychologist John Tierney and science writer Roy Baumeister explain how we suffer from "decision fatigue." Think of passing those glowing golden arches on the way home from a long day at the office and how easily the thought of just picking up a burger rather than going home and cooking pops into your head. I had just finished reading *Willpower* when my husband and I went on the South Beach diet. Our diet was very successful, but we had never been so short tempered with our children. After spending all day resisting bagels and cookies, it was beyond us to resist snapping at our kids.

The good news is that willpower and quick decision making are muscles that can be developed so that you can get better at them (i.e., you can stop snapping at the kids and still keep the weight off). And the main thrust of the second half of this book is to teach you to develop habits that are automatic, so that you don't have to make decisions when you are tired or rushing and can stop clutter problems before they start. The decision has already been made. You walk in the door and immediately put your shoes away (goodbye pile in the hallway); you pay or file the Amex bill as soon as you open it (goodbye stack on the kitchen counter); you don't even open the e-mail about the 50 percent off sale at the discount clothing store (goodbye overflowing closet).

The habits explained in this book have been the most useful to me and to many of my clients, but they aren't the only ones. Once you grasp the technique, you can develop any habit you choose. You probably already have plenty of good habits; you just weren't necessarily conscious of how you developed them. I'm often amused by clients who tell me that they are "hopeless," "lazy," or "have terrible habits." This may be true about how they deal with their piles of paper or their homes in general, yet some of those same clients are devoted to their exercise routine, religious about seeing their hair colorist, or dedicated vegetarians. All things that this gym-averse, gray-haired carnivore can't even imagine. The truth is that anyone can get into the habit of being organized!

One Habit at a Time

Studies have shown that people do best when they develop one new habit at a time. This is why when you decide that starting Monday you are going to start running, give up coffee, and keep your e-mail in-box at zero, you usually fail. A month might seem like a long time to concentrate on a habit, but to make it second nature, which is what we mean by "habit," you have to give it that much time. After you've read this section, you can decide which habit you want to work on developing first. You may decide that some of the habits I mention aren't that important to you, or you may believe that you already have established others. However you want to approach these habits is fine, but concentrate on one at a time.

Words *and* Action

Remember in the introduction, when I told you to get a notebook? Now you are going to need it. Maybe you're saying, "What kind of an organizer are you? I don't need a notebook, I do everything digitally!" Okay, if you must, you can use your phone's apps, but I've found that it's still good to have a place to take notes, because although some of your progress can easily be tracked in an app or a spreadsheet, it is only part of the story. Forming some habits can be a more fluid process. A journal can be helpful in understanding why you are succeeding or struggling.

Let's say you succeeded in getting your living room back to neutral for three nights and failed on the fourth and fifth: What happened? What's the story? Were you tired? Did you have friends over? Did you have a blowout with your teenager?

The point isn't to judge; it's to really understand what's going on so we can change our behaviors. This is why we need to dedicate a full month per habit; we need to have the experience of trying to maintain the habit on good days and bad days, lazy days and frenetic days. We need to see where we are vulnerable but keep our focus zeroed in so we can build the habit. Remember, this is an ongoing process—and, don't worry, you'll still see some significant changes pretty quickly. Even more importantly, you can carry these new approaches into every aspect of your life.

CHAPTER 8

Keep Your Stock Shipshape
Habit: Take Inventory

Inventories can be managed, but people
must be led.

—ROSS PEROT

o you know what you have? Where it is? Whether it fits?
These are the simplest, most concrete building blocks of
organization. Among my clients' worst habits: buying things
they already have because they couldn't find them. *Ouch.*
That kills me. People also have a lot of anxiety about running
out of things, so they overbuy, which leads to more clutter
and an inability to find things. A vicious cycle!

Being organized should be like breathing: things come
in, things go out. You should always have *enough* of what
you need on hand—clothes, food, paper goods—but not *too
much*. That's why you need to inventory each area of your
home. An inventory can be a jumping-off place for a grocery list in the kitchen, as in what staples you usually have
on hand. Or it can simply be what remains after a good weed
of your linen closet: one change of sheets per bed plus one
for guests, one change of towels per bathroom plus one for

guests, and so forth. Whether you are talking about white undershirts or vanilla yogurt, it doesn't matter. To *take inventory*, you need to determine how much you need to have "in stock." You also need to be clear about how much you can fit in your home and how often you shop. Your inventory keeps you honest: "Wait, I can't buy this cute tablecloth, because I already have a full inventory of tablecloths and I'm not willing to throw any of them away." With perishable and disposable items, an inventory list helps keep you organized: "I'm into the second ream of copy paper, time to get some more." Your inventory is a maintenance system that helps to alleviate the urge to overbuy, while making sure that you never run out. This way, you'll always have whatever you need at your fingertips.

Before You Begin

In time, you'll want to take inventory of every area of your home, but the easiest ones to start with are the disposables: food and toiletries, for the most part. Once you have weeded and organized, you will know what you have and what you need, and from that you will create your master shopping lists. For other areas, such as linens, you probably don't need actual lists (though if it makes you feel better, knock yourself out). It's enough to have weeded and committed to purchasing only to replace. But for frequently purchased items like food and toiletries, keeping a master list is key. Your list can be digital or paper—the point is to be consistent about maintaining it. If you have a laptop or tablet, you can take it right into your kitchen (or office or bathroom) and compile your basic grocery (or office supply or toiletry) list right there.

Before you begin, let me make a plea for simplicity. For example, I usually cook for my family five nights a week. I know there are recipes that call for canola oil, and I know that it has a higher smoke point than olive oil, and it's therefore better for some recipes. But here is the thing: I live in New York City and I have a very small, very busy kitchen, so I just use olive oil all the time. I can cook at a lower temperature. There is just nothing more annoying to me than pulling out canola oil I bought in July and discovering it's rancid. I'd rather stick to one oil and adapt the recipes. I feel the same way about my beauty products. Turns out that the jojoba oil that someone recommended for my hair is great on my skin too. Less clutter in the bathroom, and I can use stuff up before it gets yucky or sticky or old. What items can do double duty for you? Remember, one is better than two!

Set a Goal

Before you make your kitchen inventory list, you'll want to first practice FLOW in the space. Go through your kitchen pantry. If you haven't already, spend an hour pulling out cans from the back of cabinet, tossing expired food or food you just don't like. Don't feel bad. This is the end of the waste, so forgive yourself, let stuff go, and move on.

Now, think about how you eat during a usual week and what you'd like to change. This isn't the time to totally reinvent your family's eating habits, but it's okay to up your game a bit. If you usually go out once a week and order in twice, maybe make it your goal to order in only once. Or maybe you intend to take your lunch to work but tend to run out of steam midweek. You could aim to take your lunch for four days and buy it on Fridays. Some people go so far as to make a weekly menu, but personally I keep it simple. I put chicken, fish, and meat on my list every week. I change up whether it's a whole chicken or breasts, salmon or flounder, steak or pork, and somehow I seem to be able to get five dinners out of that on a consistent basis.

Decide When and Where You'll Shop

For groceries, it's important to designate a shopping day or days (my husband goes to the big grocery store on Thursday; I go to the farmers' market on Saturday). Although you won't need a weekly trip to replenish toiletries, you should establish a routine about where and how often you shop for those items. The same goes for clothing and other items, though I hope that these are semiannual excursions rather than monthly ones.

Make Your Inventory Lists and Minimize Waste

In *Decoding the New Consumer Mind,* consumer research psychologist Kit Yarrow quotes a busy working mother on going to the supermarket: "I always seem to forget something . . . or I get there and round steak is on sale, but I can't remember if I have peppers, so I buy more and I get home and there they were; now they might be wasted." This haphazard approach indeed leads to waste and clutter. It's much better to manage your pantry inventory. In fact, that's one of my favorite analogies: When I am pulling a bunch of expired cans and mealy rice out of the back of a cabinet, I tell clients to think of their kitchen as a deli or convenience store. We've all been in delis where there are a few sad-looking cans and some ancient boxes of Ronzoni on the shelf; meanwhile, the gleaming beer and soda coolers are clearly where the action is, along with the chips and cigarettes. I always wonder if it wouldn't be better for those delis to just lose the dusty stuff that doesn't move and devote more space to snacks and beer!

Of course I'm not suggesting that you stock your kitchen with beer and chips, but you should think of your kitchen as an enterprise: you want your produce to move, you want your stock to rotate, and nothing should hang around so long that it is dusty.

Now, you can take stock and see what you use regularly. Make a master list on your computer or your phone. A master list is really a grocery list that contains the items you always want to have on hand. For example, your list might read like this:

Grocery Store

- [ ] Milk
- [ ] Yogurt
- [ ] Cream cheese
- [ ] Chicken
- [ ] Beef
- [ ] Fish
- [ ] Broccoli
- [ ] Green beans
- [ ] Spinach
- [ ] Pasta
- [ ] Bagels
- [ ] Sandwich bread
- [ ] Sliced turkey

For ingredients that you are only going to need sometimes, like mustard or canned tomatoes, you will decide on a
system for putting these items on your grocery list. This could
be a Word document or a note in your phone that you add
items to as needed, a notepad on the kitchen counter (simple
and effective), or a Google doc that you share with other
members of your household. Whatever you choose, just be
consistent. In my house, we have a piece of scratch paper and
a pencil in a drawer. As I realize I need things that I don't
necessarily buy every week, like agave or chicken broth, I jot
them down. Then on Wednesday night, before my husband's
Thursday trip to the grocery store, I'll sit down for a minute
with the scratch paper at my computer and update the shopping list. At that time I might specify quantities and add a
few ingredients for specific recipes I'm planning on cooking
in the following week. One week I might eliminate chicken
because I know we are going out to dinner on Tuesday, but
it will be back there the next week so that I don't have to
think too hard. I have green beans and broccoli on my master list, and although in the spring I might substitute asparagus, I always know I need to buy a veggie. So the list that my
husband takes to the store might look like this:

Grocery Store

- [ ] Milk (1 gallon)
- [ ] Yogurt (2 chocolate, 1 large plain)
- [ ] Cream cheese (1)
- [ ] Chicken (2 lbs. breast)
- [ ] Fish (salmon, or whatever looks good)
- [ ] Broccoli (1)
- [ ] Asparagus (2 bunches)

- [ ] Spinach (baby—½ bag)
- [ ] Pasta (whole wheat rotini)
- [ ] Marinara sauce (1 jar)
- [ ] Chicken stock (1 box)
- [ ] Canned tuna (2)
- [ ] Bagels (6)
- [ ] Sandwich bread (1)
- [ ] Sliced turkey (½ lb.)

Notice that I specified some items, changed green beans to asparagus, and eliminated beef. After I send the list to my husband (or print it), I hit "Don't Save Changes" so that it reverts to my standard list for next time. If my ten-year-old daughter comes along to the store, we like to print it out because she enjoys crossing things off the list, just like her mom.

Inventory in the Pantry

When my client Alana and I emptied her kitchen cupboards, Larabars were squirreled away in five different places, while long-expired cans lingered on the back of the shelf. Alana complained that she felt like she was always running out of food for her large family, despite frequent trips to the grocery store and Costco.

We devised a dual system. She kept an ongoing grocery list in her phone that she could refer to or send to her husband or babysitter if they ended up at the grocery store, and she kept a plain-old pad and pen on the kitchen counter where all the members of her household could write down anything they used the last of. We also created a master

---

Buy the Basics

It doesn't matter what kind of food you eat; whether you're a vegetarian, an omnivorous foodie, or a steak-and-potatoes type, there are certain basic staples that are common to most diets. I always encourage people to go for "whole" foods—onions, garlic, beans, greens—and stay away from packages. Tex-Mex rice can only be Tex-Mex rice, frozen chicken fingers are only chicken fingers, but buying rice and a whole chicken gives you options. If you break what you eat down to its most basic building blocks, it's more flexible. Onions, for example, are the black turtleneck of your pantry: you use them all the time and they go with everything.

In Michael Pollan's 2008 book, *In Defense of Food,* he begins, "Eat food. Not too much. Mostly plants." It's not only healthy; following these instructions happens to be a great way to keep your kitchen organized. Not too many lumpy, Mylar-wrapped items with a long shelf life. And a bowl of fruit on the counter totally works with a life-is-happening-here aesthetic.

---

warehouse-store list on the computer, because that errand wasn't done on the fly, the way the grocery store shopping often was. The list included supplies like toilet paper and toothpaste as well as food staples she tended to use a lot of, like canned tomatoes and chicken broth.

In my house, we keep our lists by store. We have master lists for the grocery store, the warehouse store, the farmers' market, and the health food store. For example, a warehouse list might look like this:

Warehouse Store

- ☐ Toilet paper
- ☐ Paper towels
- ☐ Dish soap
- ☐ Toothpaste
- ☐ Shampoo
- ☐ Ibuprofen
- ☐ Seltzer

I keep these other lists in my phone. I do this for the health food store because I sometimes find myself in that neighborhood with a few minutes to spare, and for the farmers' market because it isn't such a long list, so it's just easy to pull my phone out of my pocket and make sure I didn't forget anything.

Building the Habit

By now you've tossed all your expired and unwanted food. You've thought about what you really cook in a week, and you have created a master grocery list and decided what format (digital or paper) you are going to use. Finally, you have designated a grocery-shopping day. Now you are ready to set about developing the habit of keeping your stock shipshape.

Our old habit might have been to just wing it at the grocery store. Let's look at what's wrong with that habit. Did we end up with too much toilet paper because we were never sure whether we needed it, so we would buy it every time? Or are we coming up short, because our kids never tell us that we are out of chips until they complain that there are no snacks? Is there waste? Lots of people are just as influenced by piles of gorgeous produce as they are by the smell of Cinnabon or the glowing golden arches of McDonald's. But if your kale wilts in the vegetable crisper and your cauliflower turns brown, then you are not really controlling your inventory very well. Making a habit of knowing what you have so you can keep your stock replenished without overpurchasing is one of the core tenets of any organized home.

During the week, you're going to work on actually cooking all the groceries you bought. I tend to cook in order of perishability, so in my house it is often fish on Monday, chicken on Tuesday, beef on Thursday. Just as we talked about FLOW in Chapter 1, I want you to think about your groceries as coming in and going out. Don't prepare for the floods. You don't want waste, so buy what you need for a week but no more.

People say, "But what if I end up having people over?" That's why we have rice, beans, and pasta. A pound of chicken can feed masses if you shred it over some rice and beans. A pound of sausage is a huge amount when you toss it into a pound of pasta. When your inventory is consistent, you will always know what you have and you will always have enough.

People also say, "But what if I see a recipe I really want to cook in the newspaper?" No problem, just put the ingredients on your grocery list. But I urge you to think twice before trying complicated recipes that call for lots of exotic items. Over the years, I have found several "good pairings." I'm not talking about a robust cabernet with my osso buco, I'm talking about two dishes that I can cook back to back to eliminate waste. For example, there's a pork salad I make that calls for several fresh herbs that are also in a pasta dish I like, so if I make one, I make the other the next day so that

I don't end up with wilting basil and mint. If I make a cake that calls for five egg whites, I'll make crème brûlée to use up the yolks. I am always trying to eliminate waste in my kitchen.

Identifying the Cue

Here's a tip about inventory: Don't wait for the cue, create the cue. Don't go grocery shopping because you have nothing in the house, go shopping because it's Monday or Tuesday or whatever day you've decided is going to be grocery day. By getting out ahead of the need, you will avoid the common pitfalls: you won't already have a house full of leftover take-out, you won't shop when you're hungry, and you'll get in a routine so you use up and replace items at a predictable rate.

I frequently remind clients to check their inventory before they shop, whether it's for groceries, black pants, or pencils. You can't know what you need if you don't know what you have. Not to mention, once you have organized everything, checking your inventory should be a quick and efficient matter.

Tracking Your Progress

If you've decided Monday is your grocery day, you need to update or print your grocery list on Sunday night. Use Monday as your start day, and mark it in your calendar. Remember, you are going to focus on this habit for one month. You might think, "Well, that's too easy, I can do this and work on my mail habit at the same time." Maybe you can, maybe you can't, but I promise you are going to have more success if you keep your focus narrow and aim for just one habit each month.

After your trip to the grocery store, everything should fit nicely in your cabinets. During the first week, focus on sticking to your plan: cooking, taking your lunch, whatever your plan was. Remember, your reward is going to be less waste, less clutter, less running out of things: better inventory management.

Perhaps the first week, you do a great job of cooking everything you bought, but you realize you underestimated the amount of bread you need. Resist the impulse to go to the store for backup. Try to eke it out. Use up those steel-cut oats you couldn't part with. If you have to go, you have to go—I don't want anyone's children starving, but make it a quick run, get only bread, and save the real shopping for grocery day.

Spend a month really trying to keep this system at the forefront of your mind. Take notes in your journal or on your calendar, adjust your master grocery list if necessary. Concentrate on getting everyone in the family on board. Repeat after me: "No, we cannot order pizza, tonight is chicken night." Like any habit, this one becomes easier. Right now, your default may be to order in when you're tired, but in a few months it may actually be easier to just throw the skillet on the stove than to decide whether to order pizza or Chinese!

Other Inventories

Once you've mastered the grocery inventory, which is probably the most complicated in most homes, you can think about other areas. For some things, like toiletries, you can

Why Disposable Isn't Efficient

If you use a lot of disposable paper goods, let me urge you to rethink this. A large package of paper napkins takes up a significant amount of space. More dangerous still, that package will shrink as you use it up. What's the problem with that? Nature abhors a vacuum. In my experience, while you work your way through a family-size pack of paper napkins, other stuff creeps into that space: some take-out containers you washed to reuse, the plastic water bottle your kid got at soccer, an apron you never wear. When we use disposable stuff, our space needs are constantly shifting.

On the contrary, a set of cloth napkins doesn't take up much room, and it will always take up the same amount of space. As we'll discuss more in Chapter 11 (page 158), having a defined amount of space (a boundary) allotted to a category makes things simpler, and if your space needs are consistent, it's easier to stay organized.

follow the same general system. For other inventories, like clothes or sheets and towels, you may or may not choose to keep a formal list, but you should spend some time thinking about what you have and what you need.

Toiletries and Medicine

Begin with a quick purge, just like you did in the kitchen. If things aren't already in good order, give yourself some categories. For example, you might have hair, face, body, pain relief, summer (sunblock, bug spray, and itch relief), first aid, and prescriptions. Notice whether you have a lifetime supply of any one category, and if you do, let some go. Think about whether you have a reasonable amount, or whether your goal should be to reduce it.

If you have thrown out expired products that you want to replace, like aspirin or antibiotic cream, start a list (or add to an existing list) in your phone now, so that next time you are at the pharmacy or warehouse store you can replace it.

With items that don't get used up on a regular basis, your cue is going to be *when you notice you are getting low.* Don't wait to run out completely, because then you'll have a kid with a scrape and no Band-Aids, but don't use a trip to Target as your cue, because then you'll have too many Band-Aids.

If your phone is handy and you train yourself to put things into your toiletry list as items run low, you can have a very smooth system.

Office Supplies

I have a client, Lia, with eight kids. In Manhattan. For real. As we worked our way through her enormous apartment, we tried to create categories: off-season clothes, hand-me-down clothes, school supplies. She had enough school supplies to stock a stationery store. By the time we had gathered them all in one place, we had hundreds, *hundreds* of number 2 pencils, still in their boxes! We also had dozens of binders—some brand new, others lightly worn—and more loose-leaf paper and highlighters and hole-punches than you can imagine.

"Why," I asked, "are there so many pencils?"

"Well, I think my husband goes to Costco every September and gets what he thinks they need," she said. She explained that it always seemed too time consuming to try to figure out what they had on hand.

Lia had saved half an hour in September, but now she was spending half a day with an organizer to deal with her glut of office supplies! This is a classic disconnect, and it is so easy to fix. First, we agreed that she would talk to her husband and make him aware of their oversupply so that they could at least stop the influx. Then, we discussed a system for how she would purchase school supplies for her children. In September, when her kids received lists from their teachers, she would first "shop" in the cabinet where we had stored all the supplies. Whatever she didn't have from the various school-supply lists, she would put together onto one list that she or her husband could take care of in a single shopping trip. Throughout the year, if her children needed anything, they would check the supply cabinet first. Eventually, some of the stock reduced, and the children got over the idea that every September meant a new binder.

Clothing

You don't have to write down your clothing inventory, though it might be instructive to do so. You should, at least, go through your clothes piece by piece and let go of the unloved, unworn, and unflattering. And, while you are putting shirts with shirts and jeans with jeans, you should be asking yourself, "How many pairs of jeans do I really need?"

People have different needs depending on their lifestyle. Some people need to dress up for work; some people love clothes and use them as a form of creative expression (I get it); others are totally happy with a basic daily uniform of jeans and T-shirts. However, almost everyone I know has too many clothes.

Ask yourself the tough questions: Am I really going to wear it? If I wear jeans only on Saturday and Sunday, do I need seven pairs? Can I walk in those shoes?

For example, a clothing inventory might contain:

6 nice tees
4 ratty but beloved tees
3 pairs of jeans
2 pairs of shorts
1 pair of casual pants
2 casual skirts
3 pairs of athletic bottoms
5 pairs of dress/work pants
3 dress/work skirts
4 work blazers
2 dressy cardigans
4 sweaters
6 dresses
10 pairs of underwear
4 bras
1 set of Spanx
2 camisoles
14 pairs of socks, various types
7 pairs of hose/tights

This is hardly a minimal wardrobe, and yet it is much less than many people have. Also, this is total, for all seasons, so if you had four blazers, two might be all-season and one summer and one winter. Now, this isn't a rule or even a recommendation—you may look at this list and say, "Well, I have only one pair of jeans," but then you may remember that you have thirty T-shirts and a drawer full of socks. This is an excellent time to think about what you really need for who you are right now.

After you winnow down and organize your clothing using the technique of FLOW, commit to using up what you have and not buying until you actually need to replace something. I'm not going to give you a shopping strategy here, because most people need to put their energy into *not* buying clothes. I'm confident that if you actually have no wearable T-shirts you will remember to buy some more: "Oh, thank god, this T-shirt has a hole, now I can *finally* buy something!"

Kids' Clothes

Kids not only use up their clothes; they also grow out of them. That's why I like to keep their wardrobes minimal. My twins have a school uniform, so they each have five shirts and three pairs of pants/jumpers and two sweatpants for school, and then they have about ten T-shirts and five pairs of pants or skirts for weekends and vacations. They also each have a few outfits for special occasions and a few sports- and activity-related items.

I generally do a sort-through with them a few times a year when the weather changes and in time to order new uniforms if they've outgrown last year's. I am also religious about going through the hand-me-downs I have stored from my older son so that I don't run around buying T-shirts for camp only to find out we have plenty in the hand-me-downs drawer.

When I go through clothes with my children and they do need something, I make a list (often on my phone). For school clothes, sometimes I just bring the laptop right into the bedroom and put together the order right then and there. But if they outgrow or wear something out midseason, they know to put it on my desk so I can order a replacement if necessary. I can determine whether it's good enough to pass on to our neighbor's kids or whether it's bound for textile recycling. In and out: the more that goes out, the better.

Specialty Items

This is the stuff that will drive you crazy: the ski helmets, the snorkeling equipment, the nebulizers. It seems crazy to throw these things out, but they are bulky and rarely used. The natural instinct is to squirrel them away in some corner closet, which is fine, but you have to know that it is there (inventory!) and be able to access it without too much hassle when you book your ski trip or your kid starts to wheeze.

You may, in fact, need some of this stuff (I'm not here to tell you to throw out your child's nebulizer!), but when it comes to expensive sports equipment, let me be an advocate for renting. Usually, the rental equipment is more up to date than what you own. Unless your family goes skiing every weekend, if you have limited storage space, you might be just as happy to not have to schlep all that stuff on the plane.

If you do have stuff you need to keep, make sure it is all clean, neat, and ready to go for next season when you stow it away—no single gloves or damp flippers. Many of my clients have a simple system: they keep all the ski gear together in duffle bags they can grab when it's time to go skiing, all the snorkeling and diving gear in another duffle bag, and so on. Some people write down what they have stored where so that they don't have to climb up into the closet and pull down the suitcase to find out if they have ski gloves up there.

The logical way to do this is either a note on your phone or a Word document that might then be stored with packing lists in a file called *Travel* on your computer. The point is to have the items accessible and organized when you do need them.

Your Rewards

As you move through your home, keep thinking about your belongings as inventory. This habit is not just mechanical; it's also a mind shift, which can be incredibly powerful. Taking stock of your possessions will help you rein in your overbuying and regain control over your stuff. For everyone, it's reassuring to be reminded of how much we really have. The rewards of this habit are twofold—tangible and emotional—you'll not only have better systems and less waste, you'll realize that, actually, you *do* have more than enough.

Remember . . .

Know what you have.

Know how much you have.

Keep your inventory constant.

CHAPTER 9

If You Structure It, You Will Do It
Habit: Block Out Time

I must govern the clock, not be governed by it.
—GOLDA MEIR

Time: Where does it go? How do we get more of it? For many of my clients, time is the final frontier. We've organized the stuff, the house, the clothes, the papers; the real issue is finding the time to maintain the systems we've created.

The good news is that you are probably wasting more time than you think, and so you *do* have the time—but first you are going to have to break some bad habits.

Blocking out time is really about inventorying your time (and if you read Chapter 8, you are now an expert on inventories). How do you know where your time is going if you are spending five minutes on Twitter here, ten minutes on Facebook there, without a plan for the day? It's like snacking when you are trying to diet—it's hard to get honest when you are having a handful of cashews here and a fistful of M&Ms there.

When you block out time, you don't just make a to-do list. You then schedule *everything* on the list in your calendar. The time you need to respond to e-mails, the time you need to work on your big project, even the time you devote to social media: if you need to do it, you put it on the calendar.

No chunk of time should be less than half an hour, and you should be realistic about how long things take—generally, longer than you think. Sometimes people find that this exercise helps them to be more efficient. Often it reveals that they were really trying to do an unrealistic number of tasks in any given day.

Chunking

Chunking, or bundling similar tasks together, is how we are going to schedule the items from our to-do list onto our calendar. Often I help clients put together a to-do list. They come up with tasks as we are going through their desks, and I act as secretary, writing down everything they remember as we go through the layers of paper. It can seem overwhelming and take up pages on a legal pad. Truthfully, though, many of these tasks will only take a minute.

Once we've come up with the main list, we go back and categorize (remember, *like with like*). Put e-mails together, phone calls together, action items together, and so on. This helps you to "chunk" your time. So you to sit at your desk and spend a half hour on e-mails: send or reply to all the e-mails you need to. Don't look at Facebook, don't make a phone call that occurs to you, only send and read e-mails. That is chunking. Then do the same thing with your phone calls.

The reason to do this is so you can block out time, rather than schedule 50 one-minute items. That would be nuts and labor intensive. Instead, we are going to build *E-mail* and *Phone calls* into our calendar and then refer to our categorized to-do list and our in-box to see what those e-mails and calls are going to be on any given day.

Prioritize

The beauty of prioritizing is that you can take a deep breath. You can say, "This report must go out today, and when that is done, I'll just keep working away at the rest." Productivity guru Stephen Covey has a great metaphor for time management. He calls your big tasks "rocks" and the small ones "pebbles." He advises people to schedule the "big rocks"—the important, time-consuming jobs—first. If you have a big project, whether it's building a spreadsheet or packing your kid's trunk for camp, you have to block that time into your calendar: "10 a.m.–12 p.m.—Spreadsheet." Then you would take your "little pebbles," like phone calls and e-mails and fill in around those big rocks. If you use this approach in conjunction with my "chunking" method, your day could look like this:

Schedule

7:00–8:00	Get kids off to school
8:00–9:00	Eat breakfast; Straighten up the kitchen.
9:00–9:30	E-mails
9:30–10:00	Social media
10:00–12:00	Big/Hard/Important task
12:00–12:30	E-mails
12:30–1:00	Phone calls
1:00–1:30	Eat lunch

1:30–2:00   Big/Hard/Important task
2:00–3:00   Next most important task
3:00–4:30   Phone calls and e-mails
4:30–5:00   Create to-do list for tomorrow and
            tie up any loose ends from today

Obviously, the tasks will differ from person to person, but prioritizing and setting blocks of time aside for the hardest, most time-consuming tasks is useful in any context. Notice that I put lunch in there. Sometimes people get so focused that they forget to eat lunch. That doesn't end well; it leads to frayed nerves, flared tempers, and candy bars. However, especially if you work at home, stopping for lunch can turn into lunch and a little bit of YouTube, and the next thing you know, a whole afternoon has gone down the drain, so I like to put it in but give it an endpoint.

A schedule like this is a guideline. As you work with it, you can revise and adapt it to your needs. It's wise to do the hardest, most stressful thing early in the day, especially if it is likely to take longer than you think. It is also good to build in a buffer—put something that you always mean to do but isn't really pressing on your afternoon to-do list. You can always re-allocate that time to a more important project if necessary, but also you might actually get to it one day because it's on the list. Sticking to your to-do list and your calendar may reveal where you are wasting time. It can also show you that some tasks require more time than you have been allocating for them.

Making Time

Laura was busy. You know someone like her: the head of every committee, going back to school for a second master's degree at fifty, super-involved with her children. Yet with all she did for others, she didn't always take good care of herself. Her doctor wanted her to get a cardio workout in several times a week, but she was having a hard time making it happen.

Exercise, bill paying, laundry—the things we aren't that excited about are the things we most need to schedule and put onto our calendars. You'll find time to browse Facebook or buy a new pair of shoes, but exercise? You need to put that on the calendar.

Looking at Laura's calendar, we identified several times throughout the week that she could change up her usual routine and get in a bit of cardio. By going out for a walk during her daughter's music lesson, instead of sitting in a coffee shop answering e-mails, she could get one workout in. By transforming what had been a weekly breakfast with her good friend into a morning walk instead, she could fit in another. This had the side benefit of making her friend healthier, too. Simply by making small tweaks and putting them in the calendar, Laura was able to squeeze two 45-minute sessions into her busy schedule.

Creating Your Calendar

First, decide what kind of a calendar you are going to use. It can be as high-tech (digital, color-coded, sharable, and capable of reminding you when a task is coming up) or as simple as you like. If you prefer, you can stick to your old-school week-at-a-glance desk diary. The platform is up to you; however, if you have been using a paper monthly calendar, it probably won't have enough room for what we are going to put in it.

Put Down the Phone

More than once a client has asked me, "Do you think I have ADD?" "Well, I'm not a doctor," I reply, "but I think what you have is an iPhone."

People aren't even aware of how much time they waste on their phones. They think they are being efficient, but they aren't. You are never going to be at your most efficient if your attention is divided. If you need to concentrate, put your phone in your bag, put it in another room, give it to your assistant. Whatever it takes. You'll be amazed at how much more you'll get done.

I consciously put my phone away at dinner, when I am writing, even when I watch TV with my family. *Be here now.* Really work on defining when you are "on" your phone and when you aren't. Don't just make it a default position: nothing is happening, so you start scrolling. If you do pick up your phone because you are bored, look at your to-do list and find something to do. Don't check your Instagram feed.

This may not be easy at first. Everyone struggles to balance the need to engage with our new technological reality while being able to sit still long enough to actually write a report or create a piece of art. We are all charging ahead, pulled by the centrifugal force of the Internet, posting content, consuming content, clicking, buying—but we *can* resist without being Luddites. We can harness the technology and make it work for us rather than just being swept along in its wake. Make a habit of putting down the phone, turning off the computer, and unplugging. It's amazing what you can accomplish in an hour if you don't answer your e-mails the minute they come pinging in.

I find it really helpful to use an online calendar. I like to see my month, my week, and my day with the click of a button. It's also great to spend time at the beginning of the year putting in any upcoming milestones and events that you can—vacation dates, estimated tax due dates, mammogram appointments. Similarly, one of my summertime projects is to download my children's schedule for the upcoming school year and plug all the holidays and half days into the calendar so they don't catch me unaware.

For a date that regularly occurs, like estimated taxes due, I set it up as a recurring event on my calendar. This way, even if the date is off by a few days, it will be on my radar. I also frequently use the "recurring" feature for weekly events like my daughter's jazz class and my son's guitar lessons, so that I don't forget them. I put my work schedule into my calendar, as well as scheduled phone calls or deadlines. If I want to commit to going to a regular yoga class, I put it on the calendar.

What appointments, events, vacations, due dates, lessons, or classes do you and your family have coming up or on a regular basis? Get them on your calendar. This is the scaffolding of your schedule. Now for that to-do list.

Creating Your To-Do List

Start by spending a few minutes brainstorming your to-do list. I find it very therapeutic to have a real brain dump when I make a to-do list. Somehow, getting it all on paper and out of my head makes it all feel more manageable.

Next, try this: Take an 8–1/2 × 11 sheet of paper and fold it in half and in half again. Now label the four sections *Calls, E-mails, Action items, Long term*. Write your to-do list tasks in each section.

Calls	E-mails
Dentist	Playdate: Ben
Jenny re: Dinner	Accountant-IRA
Plumber	Agent-Revisions
Haircut	Susie-Test prep
Mom	R @Fla. dates
Carol Smith re: Judy J.	
Action Items	**Long Term**
Newsletter	Bookshelf—K's room
Write checks	Recover DR chairs
Submit insurance receipts	Read up on colleges
Request vacation days	Trip to Mexico???
	Get massage!!!

Wait, you may be saying. What about the laundry? If there are chores that often fall through the cracks but that you really need to have happen on a regular basis to maintain order, whether that is "do laundry weekly" or "open mail daily," then go back and put those in your calendar as recurring events to remind you to do them.

Much like your inventory, how exactly you keep your to-do list is a matter of personal preference. You can write it down on paper or in a notebook or keep it digitally. Just please don't have fifteen different lists. I have a main to-do list that I keep in a notebook on my desk, but I also have a list of things that I think of when I am out and about that I keep in my phone. So if I think of something I need to do when I get home, like "call accountant," I can put it in my phone, but I can also do the reverse, and put stuff from my main list onto my phone so I can do them while I am out, like "Buy sox for B—size 7."

I keep a *Long Term* list at the back of my notebook that is more a list of goals or when-the-kids-go-to-camp kind of a list. I don't need to read: "Recover DR chairs" every day, but I know that packing the camp trunk is my cue to look at that list—'cause heaven knows that two weeks flies by.

I like to see everything I have to do on one page. As you develop better habits and you become more adept at moving through stuff, your to-do list should become shorter.

Back to the Schedule

Once you have set up your calendar and created your to-do lists, you can block out your time. Where can you plug the items on your to-do list into your calendar?

You aren't going to write "Call the orthodontist" on your calendar. You are going to write *Calls*, and then on any given day you will have your list of to-dos to refer to, chunked by type of activity. Schedule a chunk of time for phone calls. The same goes for *E-mails*. You may not get through your whole list, but you'll make a dent.

Then, go down the rest of your to-do list and see what you can put on the calendar. Which item is your Number 1 Top Priority Task?

Sometimes it is a matter of vicinity: "I'm going to be on that side of town to get a haircut, so it makes sense to drop off my necklace to be repaired." When that happens, I put it in the calendar with an alert so that when I am leaving the salon I am reminded to drop off the necklace (which is already in my bag, because I looked at my calendar first thing in the morning and put it there). Sometimes it's a matter of importance: "I have to get this immunization before I leave for my trip." Fitting your to-do list into your calendar is just like fitting anything else: it might take a little finagling and a little creativity, but you also have to be honest with yourself. If your to-do list fills up every free moment for the next three months, then you might be trying to do too much.

Everybody's situation is different. Maybe you are at an office all day and you are really working on blocking out time on your weekends, or maybe you need two to-do lists, one for home and one for work. Maybe you work from home and you need to maximize your use of the time when the kids are at school. Whatever your situation, this method is going to help you to find the time to get things done.

Structuring Time

Sarah was a young tech-savvy consultant who worked from home. She also had a strong spiritual practice, including a morning meditation. Even with this wonderful, grounding beginning to her day, she told me she never seemed to have enough time. Working from home, she constantly felt she had to respond immediately when her office e-mailed her. Ironically, if she had been writing the same reports at a desk in her company's office, she might have felt more entitled to ignore the e-mail and keep working on the report. But because she was at home in her sweatpants, she felt it was necessary to let the company know that she was indeed working. However, she was having trouble commanding the focus to do the bigger jobs like writing and analyzing data because of the constant need to weigh in on little battles.

She finally decided to break the cycle by telling her boss she that she was going to turn off her phone and e-mail alerts from 10 to 11 a.m. so she could focus on writing. Though it felt awkward to have the conversation, Sarah was glad she did. She found that not only did the writing go better, but also, as she continued to build this habit, her boss didn't e-mail as frequently and learned to "bundle" her thoughts and questions into fewer communications in the day. In the end, Sarah's attempt to become more efficient had a side effect of making her boss more efficient as well. Another example of someone else getting a residual benefit from our improved habits!

Bedtime for Grown-Ups

One of the many things I've learned from my husband over the years is the power of getting up at the same time every morning. When my husband and I met, we both worked in restaurants, and he still does. Although the rest of his schedule is anything but routine, he has found that waking up at the same time every morning helps give his days structure, so that he can accomplish what he wants to in the precious hours when he isn't at work.

I've found that often my clients with the biggest organizational hurdles also have significant sleep issues. Remember decision fatigue? When you are tired it's hard to make decisions. You are depleted and your ability to focus suffers. Sometimes sleep deprivation is just life: if you have an infant, *put this book down immediately and go take a nap.* Get organized after they are sleeping through the night. However, if the problem is you are on Facebook until 2 a.m., I urge you to change that habit first. If you think that you can't sleep more and still accomplish what you want to accomplish, think again. Media magnate Arianna Huffington, author of *The Sleep Revolution*, has made getting us to sleep better her mission, and she is definitely a woman who gets stuff done.

When you block things out on your calendar, you are structuring your time. You can change stuff, swap stuff around, but you need to have the architecture, the basic shape of your schedule. Your wake-up time and bedtime are the keystones of that structure. You don't have to be rigid, but you do want to be disciplined. I get up a little later on Saturday and Sunday than I do on the weekdays, but I tend to go to bed a little later, so I am getting the same amount of sleep on a nightly basis.

Think about how much sleep you are getting and how much you really need. Try to pick a time that you already usually get up and make that your designated wake-up time. The hard part is bedtime. If you need to get up at 6 a.m., you shouldn't be online at midnight. Pick a time that is realistic but also gives you time to unwind after you're done with the dishes and the mail and whatever else you have to do.

Your wake-up time and your bedtime are the bookends of your schedule. Now let's talk about the middle.

Building the Habit

Once you have chosen your bookends (wake-up and bed-times) and you have created your calendar and your to-do list, it's time to build the habit.

I've had many clients with long to-do lists and elaborate digital calendars, but they didn't look at them! What's even nuttier is that those same clients are constantly looking at their phones.

Identifying the Cue

Make looking at your calendar one of the first things you do in the morning. Waking up is your cue. I'm all for waking up with coffee or yoga and staying away from technology, but once you've saluted the sun and downed that first cup of joe, I know you are going to look at your phone anyway. So do it mindfully. Don't just look at your Facebook feed or all the tweets that have flown in while you were sleeping. Make it your practice to start your day by looking at what you have planned.

Tracking Your Progress

Even if your calendar and to-do lists are digital, you might want to print them out and tack them to the wall in front of you at first. Every time you finish one task you want to develop the habit of looking back at your to-do list. Say it like a mantra: "Return to the to-do list." The other great thing about printing out your to-do lists for the first few days (or weeks, whatever it takes) is that it can be very satisfying to cross things off as you accomplish them.

Research shows that when you are trying to instill a new habit, it's a good practice to link the new habit to an existing one. So if you are already in the habit of checking your phone in the morning, use that as your cue to check your to-do list. You could link this new habit to any well-established morning habit you have, like drinking your cup of tea or standing at the kitchen counter listening to the radio. Whatever you choose, you want to make establishing this new habit your primary focus for the next thirty days.

But what about the rest of the day? Make returning to your to-do list a major focus. This can be tough, because people get "in the flow" of the day and get swept along. With phones ringing and e-mails pinging, we spend too much of our lives in reaction mode, which is actually kind of crisis mode. And really, where is the fire? Yet an e-mail comes in and we leap into action. But we have more control than we think, and trying to honor our schedule, while being respectful of our coworkers, is one way we do this.

When I first started my business, my older son was a baby. Sometimes clients asked if I could work on weekends. Having spent years as an actor and waiter, my instinct was to say yes. My husband, however, objected. This seemed ridiculous to me, especially because he was in the restaurant business and worked Saturday and Sunday every week. He said that I should have a boundary, that we should carve out dedicated family time that the three of us could be together, not just passing my son back and forth like a baton as I came home from work and he left for his job. He was right. There is no such thing as an organizing crisis. Although I may have lost some revenue from not being totally available, I've never lost a client, and in the long run I think that having boundaries made my clients respect me more and made the work more sustainable for me.

Your Rewards

In *Frog and Toad*, one of my favorite children's stories, the shorter, more tightly wound Toad begins his day by making a to-do list. Shortly afterward, it blows away in the wind. The rest of the story is Frog and Toad in hot pursuit of the list, which is always carried just beyond reach. Eventually, the more reasonable Frog suggests they give up and go to sleep. "That was the last thing on my list!" Toad exclaims. He then writes it in the dirt with a stick, dutifully crosses it out, and goes happily to sleep. It's extremely satisfying to look back and see how many items we have crossed off our to-do list. In fact, when you are methodical and stick to the list, it evolves into a "done" list, and you can see how much you accomplished in a day. When you are constantly off-task, you feel like you've been running around all day but you aren't really sure what you did.

Your reward for establishing this habit is that satisfied feeling of accomplishment that you get when you know you've done what you set out to do. The good sleep is just a bonus.

Remember . . .

Chunk items on your to-do list, like phone calls or e-mails.

Prioritize your to-do list; everything can't be Top Priority.

Schedule when you are going to do the items on your to-do list.

Commit to a regular bedtime and wake-up time.

CHAPTER 10

Get Back to Neutral
Habit: Do a Last Sweep

My idea of housework is to sweep the room
with a glance.

—ERMA BOMBECK

This is such a simple idea, with such major payoff, but it is a hard one to start. *Last sweep* asks you to spend a few minutes before bed—maybe five or ten minutes—restoring order. This isn't a time for filing; it's a time to put the pile of bills you were paying while sitting on the sofa back on your desk. It's not the time to put your kids toys away—it is a time to drop anything they left in the living areas at their door (if, of course, they ignored you when you said, "And take those Legos back to your room"). The point is that if we make a habit of spending a few minutes getting stuff *close* to where it belongs, we will wake up to a basically orderly house, and we will be more apt to keep it that way.

I know it's easy to object to this idea: "But I'm tired at 11 p.m., there's no way I'm going to do that." Or "It's their mess, why should I put it away?"

148

I hear you, and I get it, but the best leaders lead by example. If you read the previous chapter, I hope that you are working on having more discipline about bedtime. Maybe you need to detach yourself from Facebook or not watch the last few minutes of your favorite late-night show. If you still watch television with commercials (and they seem to be creeping in on all streams), try my mother's trick, which was to hop up at every commercial break and do something. Not only does this make TV watching less sedentary, it protects you from those commercials that are going to want you to buy more!

Waking Up to Neutral

As I mentioned, one of my favorite times of day is when I am sitting on my couch in the living room before anyone else is awake. I wish I could tell you that I meditate, but I don't. Still, it's a form of meditation for me, sitting in the half light, drinking my coffee, and thinking about the day ahead.

This quiet time wouldn't be so peaceful if the room were a mess. I promise you, it's worth the investment to spend just a few minutes at night picking up the lone sock that didn't make it to the hamper, putting the last few glasses in the dishwasher, and stacking the papers on your desk. Whether you are married or single, whether or not you have children, and whether you go to an office or work at home, mornings tend to be stressful. Yes, it's a new day and all that jazz, but most people experience the stress of getting out the door, nagged by what needs to be accomplished that day.

When you start the day amid chaos—unwashed dishes, scattered papers, piles of this or that—you are setting yourself up for more of the same. Chaos begets chaos. You want order, calm, and serenity, so set yourself up for that by giving yourself an orderly, serene environment.

Let me be clear: I thrive on chaos; I have three children and I embrace the messy art projects, the muddy socks, and the spilled milk. I don't want to stifle their creativity, or my own, by being rigidly neat. I like to think of my day as a Shakespearean play, or a 1930s comedy, or even *The Cat in the Hat:* there is chaos and fun, but in the end there is resolution and order is restored.

Keeping Order in the Common Rooms

In Chapter 3, I told you about Deena, whose living room had become a dumping ground. By looking at it with fresh eyes, she was able to transform it into a clean, orderly space. But, for her family to maintain it, they had to get into the habit of a last sweep before bed.

Every night, when her sons headed off to bed, she reminded them to take their knapsacks and shoes and sweatshirts with them to their room. Deena had already been in the habit of reminding her kids to brush their teeth and put their homework into their backpacks, so she was really just adding a few more items to that list. In a way, she was working on upping her game.

Sometimes, the boys took some of the items but forgot others. Deena would remind them, or if they were already in bed, she'd take the stuff and put it inside their bedroom door. She tried to do this without resentment. It's hard to reconcile, but sometimes I think that if kids (or spouses or partners) have made an effort, it's less stressful to just help them out than to make a major war about it. I find it helpful to think of it as imprinting. Though my children routinely forget a few of the things I ask them to put away at bedtime, I believe that they, too, benefit from the clean slate that is our living room in the morning. Hopefully, somewhere in their heads they are getting the idea that that is how a living room should look.

Before Deena went to bed, she spent a few minutes gathering her teacup, folding the throw blankets on the couch, and putting the remotes back in the basket on the side table. Developing this small routine meant that Deena could hang on to the improvements she'd made in her living space and enjoy her morning coffee in a peaceful and calm room.

She also found a side benefit of this new habit: the whole family's morning routine was easier. There was less "Where's my homework?" and "Where are my gloves?" Everything had been put away the night before, so morning was stress-free.

Getting Set for Tomorrow

For Sarah, the time-challenged consultant who learned to block out time (see Chapter 9), the last sweep was also a good way to prepare for the next day. Sarah worked at home, and, because she often worked until her husband got home from his job, she didn't always leave her desk in an orderly fashion. She'd abandon whatever project she was doing to go cook and eat dinner with her husband and never really go back. This was perfectly reasonable, because she had been working all day, but because her cue to stop working was hearing her husband walk in the door rather than a set end time, she didn't take time to prepare for the next workday. Nothing ever really felt "complete."

The last sweep Sarah needed was to return to her desk before bedtime and spend five minutes straightening out her papers and getting ready for the next day. We decided her cue for last sweep would be when she and her husband turned off the lights in the living room and headed toward the bedroom. She would detour into the office for her last sweep. She would not check or answer e-mails or do any work. She just had to take a few moments to make a little order on her desk, save and close out of any windows still open on her computer, and jot down anything she wanted to remember to do first thing in the morning. It took some discipline to not start working, but Sarah found if she didn't sit down, she could wrap things up in just a few minutes without getting sucked in. Not only did Sarah find it more inspiring to come into an orderly work environment in the morning, but she found that she slept better at night than when she just abandoned her desk and never set it to rights. Her reward was that she could go to sleep without feeling that work was hanging over her and knowing that, when she woke up, her to-dos were clearly lined up for her.

Last sweep is like a reset button. You put your space back to neutral—not perfect but not chaotic—so that you start the next day in a good place. You can use this method on your kitchen, your desk, the living room, or anywhere else—whatever area will benefit from a little routine TLC.

Building the Habit

Before you can establish this habit, you need to think about what a "neutral" state is for your home. Neutral isn't "the-in-laws-are-coming-for-dinner" perfect, but nor should it be heaps of clothes to the left, spilled papers to the right, dirty glasses everywhere. Neutral should be a good starting place: everything back to its home. If there are still items that don't have a home, you know what you need to do: go back to

First Sweep

In her book *The Happiness Project,* Gretchen Rubin advocates making your bed in the morning as a key to happiness, and although it may seem simplistic, I do think that when your bed is made and there are no clothes strewn around, your bedroom instantly becomes a peaceful place to rest and recharge, rather than a dumping ground that causes stress. Consider making your bed every morning a first sweep. Returning to neutral will help your home run smoothly and avoid blockages and stagnation.

FLOW. Ask yourself whether you need it, let it go if you don't, and find it a logical home where you will be able to access it if you do.

- If you have newspapers or magazines, put the excess in recycling and make a single neat stack of current issues on the coffee table.
- Same with papers—place them back on your desk in one neat stack.
- Laundry goes in the laundry basket or hamper.
- Remaining dishes are washed and set out to dry or in the dishwasher.
- Coats are hung up.
- Toys are gathered up and brought back to the kids' rooms.
- Purses and backpacks should have a spot they live in overnight.

This checklist may sound obvious, in which case a last sweep will be easy for you. Or maybe the routine sounds impossible, in which case it is worth doing and it will get easier. Trust me!

Remember, last sweep is not a time to clean the whole house. The goal is simply to make the common areas presentable. It doesn't take that long to scan the living room, dining room, entry area, and kitchen to make sure stuff isn't lingering. Last sweep should take fifteen minutes at the most, and five to ten minutes is optimal.

Organized Enough Bags, Briefcases, and Totes

- Choose a place your purse or briefcase lives—it is up to you, but be consistent. Mine lives on my desk.
- Children's knapsacks should either be lined up in the hallway/mudroom ready to leave again in the morning or kept in kids' rooms overnight.
- Recurring-use bags, like gym bags or swim bags that might be used weekly, should also have a dedicated home, either a hook in the bedroom closet or the coat closet.
- Bags that aren't frequently used, like computer cases or overnight bags, should be emptied and put away immediately after use.

Identifying the Cue

Hopefully you have established a bedtime (see page 143), so now you need to back it out by a few minutes. If bedtime is at 11 p.m., and you need to be brushing your teeth at 10:45 p.m., then maybe you want to start your last sweep at 10:30. Whatever it is, choose a time, or an event, like the end of the show you watch, and make that your cue. It is always easier to establish a new habit when you link it to a well-established one. So if you already have a good routine of brushing your teeth or putting your cell phone on the charger, think of the last sweep as simply another step that you are adding on before the already-established habit.

Tracking Your Progress

Now, just like with the previous two habits, really concentrate on this one for a month. Make a note in your calendar when you start to build this habit so you can keep track of how you do. Are you forgetting to do the sweep? Is it easy to do on weeknights, but harder on weekends? Is it too much to do in fifteen minutes? Take note of all these things, but don't give up—keep trying for a whole month.

You may discover areas of your home that still need a deeper weed or more organization because they don't really have a neutral that can easily be achieved. We'll talk more about setting boundaries on your space and establishing a home for items in the next chapter (page 158). But if that's the case, schedule a block of time to practice your FLOW on that area (see page 7). Once you've established what a neutral state is for that space, then you can start building this habit. You can continue to practice the last sweep in other areas of your home, but for the areas that are still disorganized, hold off. You can't do a true last sweep until you've gotten the room or area into the condition that you want to maintain. So if you still need to organize, put it on your calendar: "Practice FLOW on the kitchen," then once you've accomplished that, you can implement last sweep.

A Note about Other People's Spaces

Getting back to neutral is great for any room in your home. However, you can't control the other members of your household. Do your children resist your organizing efforts? So do mine. When my children were little, I did a last sweep of their bedrooms at night. (In fact, when my oldest was little, he had so few toys that I used to return his alphabet blocks to their wagon *in order*. Absurd!) Those days are gone. Although I have been trying to help my daughter, who is particularly challenged by her clutter, on a nightly basis, my general strategy now is to *stay out*. They need to get stuff off the floor and straighten their desks once a week so we can clean, but I try not to micromanage.

The same goes for a spouse whose office or closet might not be to your standards. Come up with a few ground rules (i.e., no food in the bedroom or no clothes on the exercise bike), but after that let it go. Keep your side of the street clean and hope that one day it spreads. They'll get it eventually!

Your Rewards

The rewards you reap from a last sweep should be immediate: you'll wake up to a neater home, knowing where to find what you need in the morning without stress. The more you work toward this habit, the easier it will get.

If you've ever taken dance or yoga, or even played baseball, you know that neutral is the easy but at-the-ready position that you train yourself to make your default. Similarly, when you are driving a stick-shift car, neutral is "ready"— the ignition is on, but you aren't yet driving. The great thing about neutral is that you can go anywhere from there.

Once you are consistently getting your space back to neutral, it's not only going to be easier to see where you still need to work on organization, but the bigger projects will be easier to navigate, too—like cleaning up for a party, getting ready for a renovation, or even moving to a new home.

Remember . . .

Returning to neutral sets you up for a good day.

Spending five to ten minutes on last sweep is optimal. Don't clean, just restore.

If you can't find neutral, it is probably an indication that that area needs further organizing.

CHAPTER 11

Healthy Boundaries, Healthy Homes
Habit: Set Limits on Stuff

The difference between stupidity and genius
is that genius has its limits.

—ALBERT EINSTEIN

All organizers will tell you, "A place for everything and everything in its place." That's a good start, but there is something important missing from that maxim: the place needs to be *finite*. When you are returning your rooms to a neutral state, you will be putting things in the places you have designated for them. But if a category of stuff grows too large, you can't squish those extra items into the cabinet. You can't force them into the drawer or jam them on the shelf. Nope. You have to weed.

Can I tell you how many lovely homes I've seen where, squeezed in between the beautiful matching Land of Nod dresser and bunk bed, there is some plastic drawer unit crammed with junk? That's why I encourage my clients to work backward—not "Where can I fit this?" but "How much do I need to let go of to make my important stuff fit?" You have to make decisions about allocating space: "All my good china needs to fit in this cabinet," or "This side of the closet is for my son, this side is for ski clothes and off-season storage." We tend to let things evolve, but sometimes when you don't have a plan, you don't realize that one category of stuff is acting like a parasite and eating up all the storage space in your house.

In order to develop the habit of *setting limits on stuff*, our stuff has to have boundaries. And to set those, we have to get organized. Remember FLOW?

1. **F**orgive yourself.
2. **L**et stuff go.
3. **O**rganize what's left.
4. **W**eed constantly.

Defining boundaries means that when your home is at neutral, every category of stuff, whether it's paper, clothes, or groceries, has a place that it belongs and it *fits*. If it doesn't fit, you need to go back to step 2 and let more stuff go. Once you really think you have let go of everything possible and that your problem is storage, you can take action on that. Maintaining those boundaries is really putting weed constantly into action, making it part of your ongoing routine.

Defining Your Personal Boundaries

Each situation is different. I think that for most people, a closet, a dresser, and a portion of a coat closet should be sufficient storage for clothing. However, I have many clients for

How to Choose Storage

I've seen a lot of storage solutions in my career, from cheapo plastic shelves to basic bookcases to high-end custom closets. Here are a few of the general lessons I've learned:

1. **Make a plan.** Assess what storage you need for the items you have, and have room for in your space. If you have to, wait a little while and save up so that you can make your vision a reality. For example, if you have room for four bookshelves on a wall, get four. If you get three now and need another down the road, it might not be available, or it might not match. Don't be cheap; be methodical.

2. **"Expensive custom" isn't always better.** I've seen some custom-made teak closet drawers that were beautiful but too small for two stacks of shirts and too big for one stack. And don't even get me started on one client's custom-built file drawers that didn't fit the file folders! The retail brands know what they are doing—you don't have to spend a jillion dollars to get good storage.

3. **Don't box yourself in.** Taking advantage of vertical space is a good thing, but make sure you don't go overboard. I've seen rooms where it felt like the floor-to to-ceiling shelves on all sides were going to crush you. Generally, shelving or built-ins on one wall per room is all you want.

4. **Aim for consistency.** Sometimes people have three of one type of storage box and two of another. Whether you are trying to stack them in a closet or they are on display in your family room, having the same shape and style is going to be more functional and more aesthetically pleasing.

5. **Weed more.** Don't ruin your well-designed room by squeezing in additional pieces of storage. Either swap out a too-small dresser or desk for one that meets your needs or get rid of more stuff.

whom this is not nearly enough. They require multiple closets for their wardrobe—and there is nothing wrong with that. The point is to commit to what you decide is your storage space and not to let it overflow. This is true for every area: files, office supplies, arts and crafts, toys, clothes, toiletries, kitchenware, pantry items, utility, and any other category you can think of. Sometimes it becomes apparent that there is a category you have—paper, for example—that you don't really have storage space for, in which case you need to get some.

I'm often struck that my clients have so much stuff that they have trouble wrapping their minds around it. Creating a dedicated home for a category of items and setting a boundary not only gives you a *cue* as to when you are overflowing—and hence need to weed—it also helps you see in one glance all of what you have.

Let's say, for example, you have decided to keep all of your paper party plates in the hard-to-access cabinet above the fridge. Next time you have a party, you don't have to worry, "Are there some in the garage? Maybe I put some behind the lunch boxes?" You'll easily be able to check your inventory in one move, because the plates are all in one place, not squirreled away in various corners. And you will check your inventory before you head off to the party store, because you actually might not need more.

Why Boundaries Are Healthy

If you have ever watched even five minutes of daytime television talk shows, you probably know that boundaries are healthy. There's a lot of talk about saying no to your boss and not letting your kids take over your life. All of that is well and good, but I would add that it's equally important not to let your *stuff* take over your life. Just as it's healthy to turn off your cell phone and not be constantly available, it is also healthy to declare, "I have enough. No more."

Sometimes I'm with a client and we will get an area nearly squared away, and I might say, "Look, I got all of these toiletries to fit under the sink, but it would be better if it wasn't so crowded. Why do you have six bottles of shampoo anyway?" Often there isn't a compelling reason—maybe they once stocked up on shampoo during a sale but now they don't like that brand as much. Still, it feels "wasteful" to get rid of full bottles. Remember the deli analogy? If you're using limited space on too much of something, you have an inventory issue, which is causing a blockage. Blockages aren't healthy. We want *flow*.

Don't be afraid to use it or lose it. I encourage many of my clients to go on a "buying diet." Now is the time to use up any perfectly good stuff you don't want to throw out. The idea is that we are at maximum capacity and that there is only going to be less, not more. I am a girl who likes a mission, so if I ever have too much of anything, I like to make using it a minigoal: "I'm not going to buy any skincare products until I use up the stuff Katie gave me for Christmas and the fancy freebie I got at the department store." The truth is, if you really don't like the product, you should throw it out, and if you do like it, use it up!

Tetris

One time a client said of this habit, "Oh, it's like Tetris!" I'm not much of a gamer, but I know that I like this part of the process because it's a challenge: "Here is a huge pile of office supplies we've gathered from all around the house. Now our task is clear: we will weed and then try and fit it all back into this cabinet in an orderly fashion. Go!"

As you are putting things away, remember, they won't stay orderly if they are hard to access. It's great to use the whole space, but not if you can't get at what's in the back. Sometimes you'll realize that what would be optimal, say, for your sweaters, would be a taller, shallower cabinet. For the time being you might have to do a seasonal switch, moving the heavier sweaters to the back and bringing the summer ones to the front, but put the dream cabinet on your long-term to-do list and wait for the moment when your budget allows you to replace it.

Defining Boundaries in the Closet

How much clothing do you need? Less than you have, I bet. My client Jana (who misplaced her off-season clothes for a few seasons) had a lot of clothes. *A lot.* There are some great benefits to wearing the same size for fifty years . . . but it definitely presents some challenges, especially if you love to shop like Jana does. My goal for her was clear: No storing clothes in the attic, no storing clothes in suitcases, no storing clothes in baskets. Clothes belong in the dresser or in the closets.

Shortly after we started our work together, Jana's daughter finished graduate school and moved away to her own apartment. This gave us the opportunity to use one of the two closets in her daughter's room for Jana's off-season clothes. It took a lot of weeding, but now Jana has a system. Everything in her dresser stays in place year round, but clothes in the closet (including the small shelves of sweaters and T-shirts) get switched each spring and fall. The date is scheduled on her calendar, and every switch is an opportunity to purge. Jana knows she has adequate space, and she also knows her clothes get wrecked when they are too smashed in, so she is inspired both to restrain her impulse to buy more and, when she gives in, to get rid of something old.

It isn't enough to organize our storage: we have to consciously decide what belongs in it, and then stick to that. *Define and maintain boundaries.*

Defining Boundaries in the Attic

Laura (who blocked out time for cardio walks) had a habit of overbuying, which threatened to drown her gorgeous Manhattan apartment. I thought we were making progress until I went with her to her beach house and saw the attic there. She had simply delayed the inevitable by hauling stuff from the city to the beach. Finally, it was time to say good-bye to old holiday cards, party decorations, and extra wallpaper from several renovations before.

Once we had winnowed her cache of things worth saving, we created zones: photographs, memorabilia, decorating (extra wallpaper, tile, and fabric that were currently in the house), and so forth. Everything was sorted into clear plastic Rubbermaid tubs, which we labeled, on both the short end and the side. We used large labels and a marker, which is easier to see than a small label. When we were done stacking the tubs in her attic, there was room in them to add a little bit in each category, but only so much.

The rules going forward were "No blocking the aisles. No teetering towers." If it didn't fit, she had to let go of something else in that category.

In Praise of Hooks

Why do people drape clothes over chairs and exercise bikes? Because the clothes aren't really dirty yet they aren't really clean. Sometimes you wore a pair of sweatpants for only a few hours, from when you got home from work until bedtime, so you don't really need to put them in the dirty clothes, but it seems kinda gross to put them back in the drawer—so you drape them. Let me suggest the lowly hook as a solution.

I consider hooks to be "pending" for clothes. Can't put it back in the drawer but not dirty? Put it on the hook. Then you'll wear the same pair of sweats tomorrow night, and then maybe they'll be ready for the laundry basket. Of course, if there are ten things on the hook, it's merely replaced the exercise bike, but if you are purposeful and thoughtful about it, a hook can be a great solution.

Defining Boundaries in the Kids' Room

Abby lived in a small apartment with her young son. Her large extended family doted on him, which meant that he had too much stuff. Her original idea was to get a shelving unit that would hold six 11-inch pop-up cubes from Target to house it all.

There were several problems with this idea: First, it wasn't really big enough to store all of what he had. Second, the unit was low quality, and with an energetic small boy around it would fall apart in no time. Third, the unit wasn't versatile; the bins would hold only small items like small cars and plastic animals but not larger items like trucks and his Fisher-Price barn.

My suggestion was to spend four times more to have a local cabinetry shop build her a bookshelf that would take up most of the wall. It would be higher quality and more durable, and as her son grew the shelves could hold board games, books, and trophies, rather than building blocks and trucks. She could still buy a few bins that would fit on the shelves to corral small toys and action figures, but, by spending more up front, she would have a storage solution that would last forever, instead of having to reinvent it in a year's time.

Building the Habit

Now that you have decided what goes where and you have created space and boundaries for all of your possessions, you need to develop the habit of keeping it that way.

To be honest, this is a harder habit to develop, because it isn't necessarily going to come up every day. You will quickly realize when you have been overbuying dish soap, and it should be relatively painless to remediate that behavior, but toiletries or office supplies can creep up on you because someone gave them to you or you strayed from your shopping list when you were replacing printer ink—and suddenly you realize that you are overflowing again.

You are going to have to be both strict and gentle with yourself on this one. It sounds contradictory, I know, but here's what I mean: You defined your boundaries, *good*. You set up your storage and made everything fit, and you are committed to keeping it that way, *good*. After all, you don't want to junk up all that good work you did. However, you had some bad habits—maybe you frequently brought home freebies or went impulse shopping—whatever your bad habits were, you are working on altering those behaviors that bring excess into your home. But you are human, you will probably slip, you may not even realize it until you suddenly notice that your hosiery drawer is overflowing, and you suddenly remember picking up those purple tights on sale. Forgive yourself, but note it, take it in. If you take a moment to really think about how you ended up (again) with an overflowing hosiery drawer, the next time you are confronted with some item on sale that you don't really need, you'll remember: "I don't need that. I'm not buying it." I've actually been known to talk out loud to myself in a store, "I'm just returning the shirt for Henry. I'm not shopping, just returning."

Identifying the Cue

Your cue needs to be the moment of acquisition, whether it's accepting the offer of a nice work suit from a friend who can't wear it anymore or the impulse purchase of yet another hair product. Of course, if you are sticking to your inventory, you may have made great progress in this area already.

Creating boundaries and setting limits can be a life-altering habit. Many of my clients don't realize how deeply they crave plentitude. "I have enough" is a hard concept for them. When I say to them, "You can fit two backup dish soaps under the sink, and that is enough," they don't like it. When I say, "Okay, we've made your T-shirts fit in this drawer. Now you can only buy one if you get rid of one," they feel deprived. Once they realize they have enough, they can begin to change, but it's hard to alter such deep-seated emotions. We need to take a new approach; we need to see that by setting limits we will be able to find what we need when we need it, and our belongings, whether it's a screwdriver or our lingerie, will stay nicer because we aren't jamming things in.

Tracking Your Progress

Unlike some of the other steps, I don't think you need to concentrate on setting limits and maintaining boundaries alone for thirty days. Doing it in conjunction with last sweep might make sense for some people. What you want to do is go about your life with a new awareness. But although you don't need to work on this one *exclusively* for thirty days, it's important to pick a day to start this habit. I recommend using your notebook or your digital diary to record your progress and your feelings, because this is a habit that can stir up some feelings. If you have taken before-and-after pictures of your space, you can use the after photos as a guidepost to make sure you are staying on the beam. This is an ongoing step; you aren't going to do it perfectly every day, but you are going to hold yourself to this goal and it will get easier with practice. Once you've made your drawers and storage spaces effective as boundaries, it will take only a few minutes to straighten them up if they start to slip. Maintaining boundaries isn't only about making things fit in an allotted space; it's about keeping them nice— no overstuffing! The good part about this is that if you are diligent about maintaining boundaries, you will realize immediately that you have slipped. You can say, "What happened? All the dental stuff was fitting in this drawer. I guess I have room for only two backup toothpastes, not three."

There are times, too, when your storage needs may change: your children get older and their clothes get bigger and their toys get smaller, or you go digital and require less file space but you take up knitting and need more craft space. When these things happen, you have to think them through and get creative. Can you empty a drawer and use it for knitting supplies? Can toy storage be repurposed for clothing? The point is to put some thought into it. I always advocate trying to make do with what you have first. Sometimes you will try repurposing and it won't work (Lego storage may not be so great for T-shirts), and you need to buy a storage solution. Remember, if you have to go buy something, don't be cheap, do it right. I've seen so much storage equipment thrown out because people were going for a quick fix, only to have to start over.

Your Rewards

You are the boss. You've defined your boundaries, set your limits, and now it's your mission to maintain them. Commit to your choices. Don't get discouraged if you slip, just straighten it out and note where your defenses are weak and your barriers permeable so that you can shore them up. Your reward will be twofold. Not only will you know where things are because everything has a place, but also your home is going to look great because you have fought that pesky habit of adding more storage at the drop of a (new) hat. As an added bonus, you may end up saving money once you realize just how much bug spray and how many blank notebooks you actually have.

Remember . . .

Everything needs a place, but that place needs to be finite.

When things overflow their boundaries, weed more.

If your storage is maxed out, don't acquire unless you also let go.

Put thought and effort into your storage; avoid cheap, temporary solutions that will end up in the landfill.

CHAPTER 12

You Get What You Pay For
Habit: Buy Less but Better

Less is more.
—MIES VAN DER ROHE

f I could wave a wand and magically impart one habit to all my clients, this would be it. After sixteen years, I can't tell you how many jumbo Hefty bags of stuff I've thrown out. As my husband and children can attest, my job has turned me into a rabid anticonsumerist recycler and composter. Everything is too cheap and we all have too much. "Well," you might think, "easy for you to say, your clients are affluent." In fact, I live in upper Manhattan where the last of the middle class lives side by side with wealthy families and lower-income families alike. I've worked in homes of people from a wide range of backgrounds, and guess what: it's universal. Almost everyone has too much stuff.

Although I love a bargain as much as the next gal and I celebrate the enormous variety of choices available to us, even inexpensive stuff if frequently purchased can add up to a lot of time and money spent. A shirt is only fifteen dollars, so you buy it in three colors. Before you know it your closet is bursting with cheap shirts, and eventually you throw them out. When you have clutter and you are in the habit of buying a lot of cheap items, the instinct is then to get a cheap storage solution for them. You get some plastic drawers or a particleboard shelving unit. Inevitably these fall apart and you throw them out too, because, hey, after all, they were cheap. And then it's on to the next. Pretty soon we are on a hamster wheel of consumption.

It doesn't just affect our homes. I love to share the You Tube video *The Story of Stuff* with my children and with my clients, too. *The Story of Stuff* describes the journey of consumer goods from start to finish and shows us how even if we aren't paying very much for that cheap radio, there are very real costs, to the environment and to the health of the factory workers, to name just two, being paid for our goods.

So develop this habit: *buy less but better.* It'll save you, and it might save the world, too.

What do I mean by "less but better"? I want you to acquire fewer items. I want you to think more long term and choose better quality when you do buy. And I want you to love what you own more.

When I was young, I wanted to be an actor. Grown-ups were constantly trying to scare me out of pursuing a life in the arts by warning me that I wouldn't be able to have the creature comforts I'd grown up with if I went down that path. Far from scaring me, I took their warnings as a challenge. When I left home for acting school, I felt I was taking a vow of poverty. I was determined that I would be able to live with less and, with the arrogance characteristic of eighteen-year-olds everywhere, also that I would do it beautifully, artistically, stylishly. This meant I had a futon and a single artfully arranged bookshelf.

By the time I started my organizing business, life had changed: I was in my thirties, married, and pregnant. I like to tease my husband and tell him that he has made me soft. When I met him I had a single futon without a frame, no air conditioner, and no television. Now we have a king-size bed *with a frame,* several air conditioners, and a flat-screen TV, though only one for a family of five is pretty good. Of course, it was good that I had relaxed a little bit, and, in the period when I got married and had my first child, I became more of a consumer.

Luckily, when my son was just a few weeks old, I got one of my first big clients, Leslie, who you met in Chapter 1, and for me she was like the Ghost of Christmas Future. Leslie was my age, and her newborn daughter was almost the same age as my son. However, she had two older sons as well. When I saw all the stuff that she had for her children, it was a real eye-opener. Immediately, an insecure part of me thought, "Uh-oh, do I need that? Should Henry have a bassinette and a Diaper Genie and a baby wipes warmer?"

But as I saw how much Leslie and I were throwing out, and how much of her precious maternity leave she was spending with me deciding which plastic junk to chuck, I reconsidered. I decided my baby is fine with less stuff. He doesn't know the difference. He doesn't seem too traumatized by cold wipes, and I'm going to be better off if I keep it simple.

Even armed with that knowledge, that intention, and not very much money, it has still been an uphill battle to keep my home uncluttered as my family has grown. The more I help clients let go of stuff, the more convinced I've become that *less is more* is the key.

Less but Better: Clothes

Marni, a physician with two children, was appalled when we went through her clothes. Not only did she see how much money she had wasted; she saw that the lower-end stuff barely made it through the wash. Yes, it was fun to buy a trendy new top from H&M . . . but after a few washes it was downgraded to a weekend shirt, and really—how many weekend shirts did she need?

In her excellent book *Overdressed: The Shockingly High Cost of Cheap Fashion,* Elizabeth Cline takes us through the history of clothing manufacturing to where we are today. She points out that although we spend a smaller percentage of our income on many more pieces of clothing, the clothing is of much lower quality. Because fewer people sew, they are less able to discern high quality from low quality. And, in fact, many higher-priced brands are manufactured in the same overseas factories as bargain brands, perhaps with better-quality materials, but with no better workmanship.

Marni realized that if she wanted to maintain a professional appearance, she was going to need to spend a little more per item but that it would even out once she started buying less. This was also going to make everything fit in her closet (define and maintain boundaries) and save her from spur-of-the-moment shopping expeditions.

"Okay," you say. "I get that it might be better for me to have a few really great pieces and not so much cheap stuff, but what about kids?" I hear you, and, believe me, I am not breaking the bank dressing my three kids. The key to buying for kids is to concentrate on the *less* part of less but better. Don't overbuy, accept hand-me-downs sparingly, and know that clothes are supposed to protect us from the elements, not showcase how hip our parents are. (Honestly, dressing kids up is often much more for our own pleasure than theirs.)

I've noticed that many of my clients will take a party dress from a fancy children's boutique and pair it with a white cardigan from Target. I think this is great, until I look in the closet and see that they not only bought that white cardigan, they bought it in all six colors. Because it was so cheap, so why not?

The same approach goes for trendy items: if you want to buy something trendy, fine, buy it cheap, but buy *one* infinity scarf, not five. Think of trendy items (and this goes for your tween, too) as hot fudge sundaes: okay once in a while but not something you want to make a habit of.

If we are careful and conscious in our purchasing, we will bring in less, and it will be easier to maintain order.

Why Are We Buying?

For several of my clients, shopping is a social activity. We'll do a huge weed, and things will be fitting very nicely and I'll think they've really made progress, when suddenly there will be a huge influx, sometimes of clothes, other times of housewares or home furnishings.

I've asked, "Why? I thought you said that you had plenty of clothes, and you weren't going to buy any more."

For one client, it's one of the few activities she and her daughter really enjoy doing together, and yet she frequently ends up giving away the clothes she buys on these expeditions because she finds that once she is back in her own apartment the clothes seem too young for her.

Another client, Betsy, has a habit of shopping with a good friend, but, again, the purchases from these jaunts often end up in the donation bag. One day when we'd put yet another batch of expensive, trendy blouses in a bag for charity, I happened to notice a picture on the bookshelf. "Is this Sheila?" I asked. When my client confirmed that the photo was indeed her shopping buddy Sheila, I laughed. "All those tops are her style, not your style!" Although she admires Sheila's style, it isn't Betsy's style, but until we noticed and named it she wasn't really aware enough to resist this subtle peer pressure.

For other clients, online shopping is addictive. The evolution of Internet shopping and the sophistication of retail marketers is incredible. In *Decoding the New Consumer Mind*, Kit Yarrow explains that control is the antidote to anxiety. Savvy Internet retailers have optimized search engines to give us a wonderful feeling of mastery: "I'm narrowing my search: black shoes, dressy, under $100, size 8. Now I can just choose among these sixty-four pairs! Done!" And that feeling keeps us coming back for more. We don't need more shoes. That delicious feeling of mastery has nothing to do with shoes.

But we don't have to fall for it. We don't have to buy it. We can aim higher.

Better doesn't necessarily mean expensive. Better can be about quality, which typically (but not always) costs more, but better can also mean better for *you*: more your style, more interesting, more flexible, better design. It's sometimes hard to find better clothes when we have to wade through so much dreck. You might have to spend more time and more money to buy fewer pieces of clothing, but that's *perfect*. That is what we want; you just have to change your idea of what a successful shopping trip is. For me, a successful shopping trip is when I stay on task and don't succumb to sales for stuff I don't need. Success is when I don't go over budget and I leave with what I came for—or I leave empty handed. A day spent with my best friend trying on dresses and not spending a dime? That's free entertainment if you ask me, not failure at all!

Not Buying It

I spend a lot of my time trying to come up with obstacles for my clients. You would think I would want to make their lives easier, and I do. But I want to create obstacles to their shopping, because in many cases that's what's causing the clutter. So I challenge my clients to a "no shopping" period of time.

In 2006 Judith Levine published *Not Buying It: My Year Without Shopping*. I found this book inspiring, because, as she documents her experiences and meditates on what being a consumer means in our current culture, she touches on many of the issues both my clients and I face. Levine mentions social pressure, the thrill of the hunt, and the desire to "upgrade," among other common triggers.

After Levine's book came out, there were scores of magazine articles in which the author would try to not shop for a month or not buy anything made in China (hard!). There was even a *Law and Order* episode in which the suspect was living a zero-impact lifestyle, which seemed very tough on his wife.

I experimented with some of my own rules: I only bought clothes that could be machine washed and I stuck to my film-noir color palette, so that everything would coordinate with everything else. I resisted the urge to buy clothes for my son, because between hand-me-downs and gifts he really didn't need very much.

If you've decided to go on a no-shopping challenge, this is an excellent time to work your way through all those hotel shampoos (or donate them to a shelter), dried beans, and multiple black turtlenecks. If you couldn't part with them back when you were defining your boundaries or letting stuff go, it's okay. Use them up now. Don't order in: make chili. Wear the clothes you couldn't part with that you never wear. One of two things will happen: you will use these things and save money, or you will realize that you are never going to use them and you can let them go. People think I am a little harsh about this stuff, like I am giving them a penance for having bought the wrong shampoo. And they are right, sort of, because I think when you just leave the shampoo in the back of the closet (taking up room) you aren't really owning that mistake. When forced to use it, you are confronting your mistake, and hopefully you will remember it the next time you are in the shampoo aisle being lured by pretty packaging. You will think, "Oh no, is this going to end up the same way that fancy Swedish conditioner did?"

Less but Better: Gifts

Giving and receiving gifts can be a minefield for my clients. They think they can't get rid of something because it was a gift, but they have too many scarves or sweaters or candles.

My favorite gifts are experiences. I just took my best friend to the ballet and lunch for her birthday, and it was a very special day. It was a clutter-free, memory-creating, arts-supporting afternoon. And we got to wear the nice clothes we own and never wear enough. To me, that's a win-win-win.

I always like to tell the story of a friend of mine who started giving underpants for gifts. She and her best friend were entering their thirties, and they had enough stuff already. They had enough clothes, and neither really had the space to acquire much more. However, they both had a weakness for expensive lingerie. Not the sexy kind, but the really, really well-made kind that don't ride up, that don't show through your clothes, but that cost more than a week's worth of Victoria's Secret.

Being nice, middle-class girls, they just couldn't justify spending so much on a pair of underpants. *However,* if they bought them for each other as a gift, it felt great. So, every birthday and Christmas, they would give each other a pair or two of those very expensive underpants. How's that for practical yet luxurious?

"Made in the USA" Christmas

A few years back I came up with the idea that I was going to buy only products made in the USA for Christmas. It seemed like each holiday season I'd bought more and spent more than the year before, and I wanted to limit my choices. My oldest son was horrified. "Mom, you do realize that there are *no* electronics made in the USA?"

Of course, it was not a bad Christmas: My kids still play with the Nok Hockey set I got them that year, if not with the boomerang. I learned a lot, and each year I have found more made-in-the-USA choices. One of the great things about shopping this way is that it forces me to go to local craft fairs and support local businesses—things I believe in but have to go out of my way to make a reality.

When you know that your jewelry is made by a woman named Lila in Brooklyn, the same woman, in fact, who sold it to you, then you are connected. You can call her if it breaks, or you can seek her out when you need a gift for your sister's birthday. If it seems expensive, you can think about what you know about rents in even the farthest reaches of Brooklyn and decide that, even if you are no Medici, buying that necklace is your way of supporting the arts. When you are buying cheap jewelry at the mall, you aren't necessarily thinking about who made it—in fact, you might be trying hard *not* to think about whose tiny hands strung those beads and what pennies they were paid if you are getting them for $4.99.

You might say, "I don't have time to schlep around to craft fairs." Don't fret. Internet search engines are getting better all the time. Whatever you've decided are your parameters— made in the USA, organic cotton, machine washable, no BPA—you can search for it and find it.

I've had great luck buying handmade goods online. Your American Girl doll can be totally fashionable—and unique— with clothes made in the USA. Not only are they handmade; they are often cheaper than the ones in the store. So that's a double win. Similarly, my daughter's Barbie dolls were transformed when I bought them some dresses made by a grandma in Wisconsin. I told my husband, "Gee, now they look like they are going to a tea party, not a bar!" Much better.

Less but Better: Furniture

I've helped a lot of people move and I've helped a lot of people living through renovations. With the rise of inexpensive home-furnishings retailers and online design magazines like *Houzz,* people get the urge to instantly redecorate their homes down to the last detail. It's always astonishing how quickly an entire new decor can emerge, from window treatments to accessories, in just a few clicks of the mouse and a few swipes of the credit card. "Well," you say, "what's wrong with that?"

A few things. Furniture is a big purchase. Things need to be measured and considered. You would be shocked (or maybe not!) by the amount of unassembled Ikea furniture

I've seen languishing in none-too-big Manhattan apartments. Just because you can afford to spend a few hundred bucks on impulse doesn't mean you should. And the pile of boxes isn't doing much for the decor either!

When people buy new stuff, they are often reluctant to let go of the old stuff, especially when they know it's perfectly good, so this creates a clutter issue. From tables to bookcases, I've seen people try to have it both ways: "Well, I thought maybe I could fit this bookcase in the hallway, because the new ones in the living room are gorgeous, but they don't really hold as much."

When people buy something because it goes with their "look," without really considering its functionality, mistakes happen. I suggest living with your old furniture for a while in a new space, and then making careful, strategic purchases as you upgrade. People say things like, "It's only Ikea. I can always buy this chair for now and replace it later." But that is time and money, and essentially you are redoing work.

And then there is the problem of style. Often, when people redo their homes in one fell swoop, they tend to go with the current fashion: rooms look great and clean and new, but impersonal. They could be a page from a catalog, and it's easy to tire of the style a few seasons later. That's when the urge to completely redecorate strikes again. By contrast, when a home evolves over time, it tends to reflect the style and personality of its occupants. When you acquire only once in a great while, you are more likely to acquire things that are meaningful to you, and, when they are more meaningful to you, you are more likely to be committed to them. Remember, slowing the rate of consumption is going to make it easier to maintain whatever weeding and organizing you have done; your goal is to cultivate a new way of being.

Building the Habit

Buying less is such an important habit, and it has the power to improve every aspect of your home. As I've mentioned, it's easier to develop habits that you practice daily, like last sweep before bed, and whether or not you realize it, you probably purchase things daily.

Hopefully you aren't buying clothes on a daily basis. Food and toiletries, however, are areas where you can hone your less-but-better habit, so that it's strong when you see that cute skirt in the window at the mall.

When you decide to start building this habit, get your notebook or your digital tracker ready to take some notes. For at least a week, write down every penny you spend. Do this the week before you begin your new habit. From gum to gowns, write it all down. You don't need to include recurring bills like rent or utilities, but you should track anything else. It will be illuminating to see what you spend, and in my experience just by tracking what you spend, you will spend less.

If you are one of these people, and I know many, who never buys anything but acquires a lot, then track that. Just because you get free stuff because you work at a magazine or your neighbor is a fashionista who finds it easier to dump bags of her discarded fashion on your doorstep rather than schlep them to the thrift store doesn't mean you're off the hook. Track everything you acquire, and start to think about the conversations you might need to have with your benefactors.

Identifying the Cue

After you've spent a week recording purchases (and acquisitions), you should start your month-long concentration on

buying less but better. Your cue is anytime you are about to
buy or in any way acquire something. In the grocery store,
practice buying less food of better quality. In the drugstore
ask yourself, "Do I need it?" Try to keep your purchases to
a minimum, and if there's something you really need, try to
keep quality in mind. "Will it last?" "Will I be throwing it out
in a month?" "Is there a better alternative?" Slowing down
and questioning each new acquisition is your new routine.

Tracking Your Progress

As the month progresses, look at your impulses to buy
things. Try Sarah Lazarovic's method (see page 30) and add
time to your impulse. Don't buy anything right away. Wait.
Give it a day. Check your closet, your kids' closets, and your
heart. Do you really need it? Is the old one really unwork-
able? Can you fix it? Can you rent or borrow it? Is it a want
or a need? If it is a want . . . resist.

Try this: Make three columns on a piece of paper. In the
first column, write down what you need. In the second column, write down things that aren't strictly necessary but are
important to you, whether that means fashionable clothes or
a stack of books. Finally, in the third column, write down
the other stuff you tend to buy, the impulse purchases like

Need	Want	Impulse
food	good pots	makeup
house	sharp suit	scarves
clothes	new phone	accessories
comfy shoes	face cream	herbal remedies
computer	bike	high-heels
reading glasses	scented candles	

fancy face creams or silicone muffin trays. Keep this list in mind. Buy the things you need, when you need them; take time and contemplate the "wants" before making a purchase; and keep away from the impulse items.

Your Rewards

You are building muscles here: resistance muscles. It's difficult at first, and you may slip—it's hard not to in our consumer culture—but this is a habit worth building. Remember your goal: less clutter, less chaos, less waste, more joy, more serenity, more beauty. These are rewards worth striving for. You are going to buy less; you are going to use up what you have that you can't part with. When you really have to get something, you are going to get something that will last and not be thrown into the garbage in a few months.

Less but better opens up so many frontiers. When we free ourselves from the habit of overconsumption, we are taking a stand against cheap and easy and committing ourselves to less clutter, less junk, less waste, but more beauty and more quality. And really, who wants to be on the side of the cheap and disposable? Not me.

Remember . . .

Buy fewer things of higher quality.

Develop an awareness of when you shop and what your shopping triggers and pitfalls are.

Concentrate on becoming a more conscious consumer and building your capacity to resist impulse purchases.

CHAPTER 13

Secrets of an Organizing Ninja
Habit: Ten-Minute Maintenance

First we make our habits, and then our habits
make us.

—JOHN DRYDEN

People freak out at the idea of finding ten minutes per day
to devote to straightening up, and yet they tell me how
they had to spend forty-five minutes looking for a permis-
sion slip. Ten minutes a day is an investment—it is *blocking
out time,* and it's a habit worth instilling.

For many people, the *ten-minute maintenance* habit is best
spent paper wrangling. It's amazing what spending ten minutes each day simply opening the mail, shredding and recycling the junk, and sorting what's left into categories can
do for the general organization and sense of peace in your
house.

For others, it's their wardrobe, rather than their mail, that
needs that level of commitment. Whatever your clutter hot
spot is, developing this tiny habit can yield big results.

What's the difference between ten-minute maintenance
and last sweep? Good question! Ten-minute maintenance

focuses your concentration on your toughest area every day. Last sweep is a general maintenance step. Last sweep doesn't require any thought or decision making. In my house last sweep is putting my teacup in the dishwasher, folding the throws on the couch, and tossing (and I mean literally *tossing*) any stray toys my kids left out back in their rooms. I live in an apartment, so this whole thing takes five minutes. Ten-minute maintenance requires a little more concentration and energy. In fact, it's good to think of it as a ninja-like attack on your problem areas. Because it requires energy, and focus, which tends to be weaker when we are tired, it's better to do it earlier in the day or evening, before you are totally wiped out. The great news is that, as with any habit, the more you do it, the easier it gets.

Avoidance is a major problem for many of my clients. How do you end up with a pile? It doesn't matter what it's a pile of—paper or toys or clothes—but wherever there's a pile, there has been avoidance. It's also important to understand how engaging with your hardest area *every* day can help to counteract decision fatigue.

When people avoid anything, it's usually because there are decisions to be made and they are too overwhelmed, uncertain, or tired to make them. At 7 p.m., what you want is dinner (preferably made by someone else), not to have to make a whole bunch of little decisions. So you avoid, postpone, pile. But what would you tell your kids if they failed a math test because they hadn't been doing their math homework and they think they aren't good at it? "Avoidance makes it worse, not better." Same thing applies to grown-ups. If you avoid your mail because it brings up a whole series of questions you aren't prepared to answer ("Should I switch my cell-phone carrier?" "Can we go to that wedding in June?" "Should I go see the financial adviser?"), your pile gets bigger and bigger, and sooner or later something important ("I know I saw the car insurance bill") will get lost in it. By pushing through your instinct to avoid, these decisions will get easier, you will overcome your uncertainty and resistance, and you will fill in any gaps in knowledge that you had.

Another reason that people procrastinate is that they are perfectionists. Sometimes doing it perfectly, especially if you have set up an overly complicated system, is too arduous. Remember Chapter 6, "Don't Let Paper Push You Around," and Chapter 7, "Better Systems = Less Thinking"? Those chapters were meant to help you get your systems streamlined, so they wouldn't be too complicated. Still, we all have our challenging areas, and avoiding them only makes it worse. If perfectionism is what is getting in your way, confronting the issue daily will do one of two things: it will either reveal to you that there is, in fact, a simpler, more elegant solution, or it will bring home to you that the perfectionism is a stumbling block that you need to eradicate.

Ten-Minute Maintenance at Your Desk

When I met Coco, who I introduced you to in the beginning of the book, she had piles upon piles of paper in a teeny-tiny apartment. She didn't want or have room for a file cabinet, but she needed to keep good records because she worked for herself and had a lot of expenses to keep track of.

After going through the piles and purging a lot of paper, we set her up with a big four-inch binder with pocket folders that basically became her file cabinet. It would live on the floor next to the table by the door, where she opened the mail. She could also reach her shredder and her checkbook from this one spot.

Every day, Coco would take ten minutes to open her mail and take care of every last bit of it. If a bill arrived, she paid it and filed the receipt all at once, and then put the binder back in its spot. When she had company, the binder could fit on the bookshelf, out of sight.

Coco might be one of my biggest success stories. She really focused on developing that one simple habit, and it has stuck for years now, eliminating the piles of paper for good.

Ten-Minutes on E-mail Maintenance

One issue that plagues many of my clients is their e-mail in-box. Sometimes it seems the more they try to manage it, the more complicated it becomes. They have files and spend time dragging every e-mail into a file; they have three e-mail accounts they have to check. Your e-mail time is better spent responding and making decisions so that you can hit that delete button. Spending a concentrated ten minutes on this area can turn things around.

When I say to spend ten minutes a day on e-mail, I'm not talking about the *work* you do related to your e-mail every day. I'm not talking about answering messages. I'm talking about spending ten *extra* minutes to try to stay on top of your in-box.

Ditch the Junk E-mail. As always, the first and best strategy is to stop the onslaught. Label stuff as junk and periodically delete all your junk mail. Don't fall for websites that require your e-mail address to access them. Just say no. Forget it, it isn't worth it. You probably didn't need whatever they were selling anyway. Unsubscribe from e-mail lists that you no longer want to be on or that you don't even know how you got on in the first place.

Use One E-mail Address. I see a lot of overcomplicating with e-mail. People have several e-mail addresses to separate the important stuff from the fluff, but then they have to check multiple accounts, so where is the gain? I say keep it simple, with one e-mail address. Don't use three when one will do.

Keep Folders Simple. I'm all for keeping folders within your e-mail for things you actually need to keep: work-related correspondence, receipts that you want to be able to refer back to and so forth. However, if you have so many folders that reading your e-mail becomes a game of dragging messages into various folders rather than taking action and deleting them, then you haven't helped yourself out.

Delete as You Go. I delete almost everything after I reply. If I need to check on what was said, I can go to my "sent" box and search it. The exceptions are the taxes I mentioned before and the PTA and co-op boards that I serve on for which I should keep the e-mail trails. In both of those cases, I keep things in folders so I can access them easily if I need them.

Set a Limit. If you spend ten minutes each day simply trying to keep your in-box to a dull roar, it will pay off. I'll be honest: For years I kept my in-box at zero messages, or close to it. Then the creep began: first a hundred, then before I knew it there were four hundred messages. Finally, I tackled it one rainy night, and I've been keeping it around forty, because that's what fits on my laptop screen without scrolling. I gave up on zero because my in-box acts as kind of a to-do box and a pending file. Shuffling things into a separate pending folder was annoying, and I like to see the to-dos. As always, the number you pick is arbitrary, but once you pick it, try to stick to it.

It gets easier. If you picked a goal of one hundred messages, the first week it might take you more than ten minutes to get there each night (or morning), taking time to label e-mails as junk or reply to quick messages and deleting as you go along. However, with a little focus, you'll get caught up, more e-mails will be diverted to junk or never arrive in the first place, and you will get ahead.

The benefit, of course, will be when you are looking for a particular e-mail and it's easy to find because there are only one hundred e-mails there, not one thousand.

Tools for Success

Before you embark on ten-minute maintenance, you should set yourself up for success. If your ten minutes is going to be about paper, make sure that you have set up a place where you deal with paper: at least some folders, a file cabinet or some place to store files, a recycling bin, and, hopefully, a shredder (see page 86). By this point, I hope that you have gotten all your paper from around the house and consolidated it in the one spot that you have allocated for paper management. If you haven't really had time to go through your files and purge, try spending twenty minutes a night until you are caught up. If you're really methodical, even the most daunting projects can be accomplished in a matter of weeks.

Perhaps e-mail is where you're going to focus. Ask yourself what digital files you need. I keep an e-mail folder for tax-related receipts (by year, and within that by category, so receipts for office supplies would go within the *2016* folder in the *Tax* folder). I also have files for various clients and for travel; for example, I might keep my beach-rental agreement in a folder labeled *Beach 2016* within *Travel*. Occasionally I create a new file, but mostly I aim to take action and delete. Once your system is set up, your daily maintenance should be easy.

If you're going to develop ten-minute maintenance around your clothes, make sure you have your system in place (see page 94). Do you have enough hangers for your closet (preferably of a similar style so you don't waste space putting curved hangers next to straight ones)? Is there a place for laundry? Dry cleaning? Items to be repaired? Have you weeded and put healthy boundaries in place? If you have, then you are at the point where developing the ten-minute maintenance habit will stop you from slipping back into your bad habits.

For example, do you have a habit of draping your clothes over the end of your bed or chair when you get home? Make it a practice to put them away: dirty clothes in the hamper, blazers rehung or put into the dry-cleaning bag. While you are doing that, pick up the pj's you left on the bathroom doorknob and empty your gym clothes out of your gym bag. It will only take a few minutes, but doing it consistently will keep that pile of clothes from reasserting itself on your bedroom chair.

Timing Is Everything

Your ten-minute maintenance habit for a clutter problem area requires concentration. So doing it just before bed isn't optimal. I've done it, when my children were little, and I made it work, but it's much better now that I can do it earlier. I do it right before I make dinner. The worst part about doing paper, in particular, at bedtime is that the last thing anyone wants to think about before bed is that credit card bill or that packet of forms to fill out.

I know that for some people, just before bed seems like the only free time they have. But because you are reading this book, and your whole life is getting more efficient and structured, maybe, just *maybe* you can find a tiny window earlier in the evening to devote to this. If you can, I highly recommend making this an early morning habit, or if you are home during the day, an opportunity for a midday break: let your cue be when the mail arrives. If you are cultivating this habit for clothing or a child's room, before bed might indeed be a good time. Personally, I find it much more restful to sleep in an orderly room than one with jeans draped over a chair or sneakers on the floor.

Ten-Minute Maintenance
in Challenging Spaces

My ten-year-old daughter is very creative; she is also very messy. And she *hates* to clean up. I've tried making it into a game. I've tried rewards and threats, and I'll admit, I've yelled. My conclusion is that the best way to help her is by setting an example. I'm trying to think of it not as caving in but as investing. Instead of losing it once a week and spending an angry half hour (or more) organizing her room, I am trying to develop the habit of spending ten minutes *with her* in her room after dinner and before bedtime. By making it an every-night habit, there won't be an accumulation of mess, so it won't be as hard. I also hope that by seeing her room neat and orderly every morning, she'll start to appreciate it and be motivated to put things away herself.

Whatever area is your biggest challenge, creating a ten-minute maintenance habit will pay dividends in time saved and stress reduced.

Building the Habit

To develop this habit, first you need to choose your area of focus: clothes, papers, your child's room, or any other intractable area. Even if you think you need to do papers *and* clothes (I do papers and my daughter's room), you should choose only one to start. Remember, it's more effective to focus on one habit at a time.

Have your notebook or app ready to act as scorecard. Spin ten-minute maintenance however you want. Some people are competitive and do well if they see it as a contest. Others use the notebook as more of a journal to document their progress. I think it is fine if you just put an X on your calendar (or give yourself a gold star!) to note the days when you practiced the habit. The point is to hold yourself accountable and track your progress.

Identifying the Cue

Remember, it is always great to tack a new daily habit onto a well-established one. My desk is next to the kitchen and I cook every night, so those two things are linked for me. For you, the best time to do paperwork might be the first thing when you sit down at your desk. Maybe your mornings are crazy and the best time to manage your clothing is when you get home from work and are changing into your sweats. Any choice is valid, as long as you have consciously thought about it and commit to it.

Tracking Your Progress

I like to start on a Monday, but some people find Mondays stressful and think it's easier to start over the weekend. It doesn't matter which day you choose, just commit. Now, for one month, track your successes and your challenges. Ask yourself "Am I doing it every day?" "Am I consistent about the time?" "Would another time of day be better?" Use the timer in your phone to make sure you are actually doing it for ten minutes and to keep you on task. Some people prefer an old-school kitchen timer because the ticking sound reminds them both that there is an endpoint and that they should be concentrating.

Your Rewards

By week two, I hope you are seeing some rewards: Does the kitchen counter where the mail used to pile up look better? Have you been able to sit in the chair in the bedroom because it is no longer covered in the clothes that you decided not to wear?

These are small victories, but to me they are little steps on the road to the serene home that you desire. Really take in that clean counter or that empty chair that's now available for you to sit in. These are the rewards for your dedication. They are small, everyday pleasures that can really improve your quality of life. As time goes by, you may notice bigger rewards: being on time to work because you can get dressed more easily in the morning or knowing exactly where the insurance bill is when it comes time to pay it. Hopefully, by the end of the month you can really see the difference in your home and feel the difference in your stress level.

At the end of the month, if you feel really solid in this ten-minute maintenance habit, add another if you wish. If it's still shaky, hold back until it feels well established. Don't rush it. Remember, you are taking time to build these habits because you want them to last forever.

Remember...

Spending ten minutes per day is an investment; it will save you much more time in the long run.

Lean in to your toughest area, be it clothes or papers. Don't avoid it.

Set yourself up for success by having the proper tools and systems in place before you begin.

CHAPTER 14

What Your Grandmother Could Have Told You
Habit: Cultivate Consistency

> Long-term consistency trumps short-term intensity.
>
> —BRUCE LEE

C*onsistency* is the foundation of any good habit. Without consistency we are constantly reinventing the wheel, redoing work we have already finished, and wasting time rethinking stuff we already could have dealt with. Save your flexible, changeable self for weekends and vacation; during the week, use consistency as bedrock from which you can soar.

Consistency gets a bad rap: it's the "hobgoblin of little minds," said Ralph Waldo Emerson, and "the hallmark of the unimaginative" according to Oscar Wilde. But I'm going to go with Bruce Lee and my mother on this one: for me, consistency is simply the secret of all success.

I didn't always believe this. In fact, many of the arrogant, misguided choices of my youth were totally based on the idea that I was too creative, too special, too unique to do anything consistently. I somehow thought that appearing at the same office at the same time Monday through Friday would crush my spirit. So for years I worked various jobs, in different places, and expended an inordinate amount of energy keeping track of it all because I thought I was above consistency.

Mason Currey's excellent book *Daily Rituals* chronicles the routines of famous creative people, from Voltaire to Anne Rice. In his introduction, Currey says, "One's daily routine is also a choice, or a whole series of choices. . . . A solid routine fosters a well-worn groove for one's mental energies and helps stave off the tyranny of moods." *Precisely.* If we want to get things done, keep things humming along, whether it's a novel or our household, we need to show up on a consistent basis. The idea that Currey and many of his subjects subscribe to, that consistency and routine free up your brain for more important tasks, is backed up by recent research on multitasking. Scientists have shown that we experience a mental drain when we switch back and forth from one task to another and also, as I discussed earlier, when we have to think too much about our next move. Consistency, whether it's about what we wear to work or the time of day we open our mail, eliminates the back-and-forth deliberation and the decision making, so we don't have to think about it. We just *do* it.

Balanced Living

If you have ever read a parenting book, you probably know that routine (a.k.a. consistency) is good for kids. They like to do things the same way every day. Some are more flexible and some are more rigid, but in general kids thrive on routine. My parents were pretty old-fashioned, conservative people, and there was quite a bit of consistency in my house growing up. When I was young, I imagined that I would raise my children in a different, more creative environment, and yet what has interested me since I became a parent is that often the most creative children aren't the ones with the artistic, freewheeling parents but rather the ones with the parents committed to structure and routine.

The level of freedom we have today is unprecedented, and possibly overwhelming in some ways. At the turn of the nineteenth century, you might have worked on a farm or in an office or factory. Going back further, our ancestors were more in sync with the hours of the day (up with the sun, in for the night at dusk) and with the seasons. The freedom that we have today—not only where we work but also how we present ourselves and what we do with our time—makes consistency harder. Society isn't as rigid today and people are more accepting of individual choice. When my mother moved to New York City in 1957, she wore high heels and white gloves on the Third Avenue El to her job as a salesgirl at Saks. Women "did" their hair and men wore suits. It was the age of the "Organization Man." The Organization Man was the man who conformed and was part of the well-oiled machinery of an American corporation. It wasn't the most creative, but on the upside he didn't have to start every day from scratch.

Remember the old adage "behind every great man is a great woman"? I think in the past, for many successful people, there was someone in the background keeping the hearth-fire burning. But guess what: we are living in a new age of two-career couples and companies committed to "flat organization." Most of us are shoulder to shoulder with our partners if we have them, and executives type their own e-mails. In today's world we have to be our own backup. We have to create the environment that will support us and free us up to do the fun/creative/important stuff that we really want to do.

When I finally broke down and took a full-time job, I was amazed by what I accomplished around the edges of that eight-hour day. It was almost as if a huge burden had been lifted that freed me up and (counterintuitively) gave me energy.

So give consistency a chance. Yeah, I know, it's annoying that everything your mother told you turned out to be true, and if you had just listened to her, you wouldn't have needed to buy this book, but sometimes we just need to hear it from someone else.

What Do You Mean, Cultivate Consistency?

As you go through the chapters in this book, you will hopefully be making changes: to your closets, your desk, the way you shop, and the way you think about your belongings and your habits in general. To make all this stick, to *stay organized*, you are going to have to cultivate consistency. You might think this is redundant: by this point, you are already cultivating six habits that rely on consistency. It sort of is, but this last habit takes it to a deeper level. You're in a habit-building mood, you've been maintaining your stock, structuring your time, getting your space back to neutral, and all those other good habits, but this one is a way to sharpen your habit-building muscles. This is the habit that will make building any other habit easy for you.

Cultivating consistency is about being mindful. Think of it as a companion habit to better systems = less thinking in Chapter 7. By bringing our attention to the small things in our life—where we open the mail, how we hang our clothes, when we go to the grocery store—we start to eliminate the chaos and create a safe space for ourselves.

Cultivating Consistency in the Laundry

I'm not going to tell you that there is only one way to fold your clothes—but it's important to learn what works for you, based on the type of clothing and the size of your drawers. Experiment, decide, and then stick to that: be consistent. Less thinking about folding means more mental energy for other tasks.

My client Karl, a successful musician, was horrified when he thought his extensive jean collection wasn't going to fit into his new, custom-made drawers. When I showed him that by folding the jeans into thirds instead of quarters, he could fit them all in one drawer, he was thrilled. By simply cultivating this tiny tweak, the jeans fit in the drawer, and Karl was a happy guy.

You can fold your clothes into "packets" (folding into a small, thick rectangle that stands on its edge) or into thirds, or you can roll them. You just need to be consistent so that what you put back after laundry day fits in the same drawer it was in before laundry day. If that means that everybody who does laundry in your house needs to have a folding lesson one weekend morning, then do that.

Don't make it too complicated. Stick to one fold per category. If you get too crazy and determine that you can maximize your drawer space by folding half your tees à la Marie

Kondo and rolling the rest, that may work as long as you live alone and no one else is doing the laundry or putting stuff away. But if someone else is often folding the laundry, keep it simple, or you are likely to be frustrated.

I have a habit of putting the hanger from whatever I am wearing that day to the far right of my closet. Now, when I need a hanger, I know where they are. It's a tiny thing that makes me happy every day. The best part? This simple habit takes no time at all to develop.

Cultivating Consistency in Your Appearance

I work for myself. In theory, I could wear anything I want to work. In practice, I have a uniform. It isn't rigid and it has some variation, but there are basic building blocks. Most days, I wear skinny jeans, a washable top that's nicer than a T-shirt, a jacket or cardigan, and shoes or boots, never sneakers. My wardrobe color palette is pretty narrow, everything goes with black and almost all of my shoes are black, so I don't really have to worry about matching. On weekends or days I work from home I might wear a T-shirt and skip the shoes.

It's the same with my makeup. I have a daily beauty routine: moisturizer, concealer, powdered foundation, blush, mascara, and lipstain. It takes two minutes. The only thing that is a choice is the lip color: light or dark. That's it. I don't stray from it, which not only keeps me on schedule in the morning but also helps with inventory control (I'm not going to buy the glitter eye shadow, because I don't wear glitter eye shadow).

Working to cultivate consistency in your appearance will help you in your winnowing process because you may realize things like, "Gee, I don't really wear silk scarves; maybe I don't need to devote a whole drawer to them." Cultivating consistency will reinforce the work you have done weeding and staying within your boundaries, and it will guide you when you are shopping. If you are working on cultivating consistency and you find yourself tempted by some item in a store, ask yourself, "Do I really wear long, flowy skirts? It's cute, but didn't I just get rid of one because I never wore it?"

You can even cultivate consistency about what you wear when you get dressed up. You can have a uniform of a cocktail dress, a little more jewelry than usual, an evening bag, and a pashmina. You can say to yourself: "I'm throwing out these super-high heels, because I rarely wear them and I usually regret it when I do." I want you to have fun when you get dressed up, but I know that having a basic idea of what it is you wear can alleviate the stress of "Oh, I have to go to the office holiday dinner, what am I going to wear?"

Cultivating consistency in your appearance will save you time and money, and who knows—you might even end up with a signature "look."

Cultivating Consistency in the Kitchen

"How often do you go to the grocery store?" I asked Becky (from Chapter 1) as I was pulling the sixth bag of rice out of her pantry. "Well, it depends." Not a good answer. Remember *inventory* and *block out time*? You need to have a full cupboard the day after grocery shopping, and an empty (or nearly empty) cupboard the day that you go to the store. My husband and I joke that we live like the old nursery rhyme: "Wash on Monday, Iron on Tuesday . . . " because we are so consistent about when we do the laundry and the grocery shopping. Consistency pays. We don't need to have a lot of clothes because we consistently do the laundry every Wednesday. Our cupboards are neat, but we eat well every night because we know exactly how many groceries to buy every Thursday. Cultivating consistency makes it easier for us to define and maintain boundaries and to block out time. It also eliminates decision fatigue (when am I going to go to the grocery store?) and creates a rhythm, which is an antidote to stress.

If you didn't already decide on a laundry day and a grocery day in the previous chapters, now is the time. If it helps, make it a recurring item in your schedule. At least one time per week, at the same time. It is okay if you typically do laundry on Tuesday night and you get invited to dinner on Tuesday to move it to Wednesday for one week—but make sure you do it on Wednesday and that the following week you go back to Tuesday. This is a life changer; you can't control your inventory well if you don't grocery shop and do laundry on a consistent basis.

Cultivating Consistency on Your Hard Drive

When you are looking for a document in a sea of paper it can be maddening, but if you *really* want to lose your mind, lose a document on your hard drive. Clients are constantly saying to me that they will "just scan" things that I am urging them to throw out. Although I understand that saving something digitally takes less space than saving the hard copy, sometimes I feel it's a devil's bargain. If you don't love it or need it enough to save the actual hard copy, maybe you don't need to keep it at all. Furthermore, I have clients who save every-thing, *everything* on their computer, then their computers are slow or crash or generally act up, at which point they get a new computer (but save the old hard drive, which takes up actual space). Sometimes they store everything in the cloud. Which is fine, I guess, but after a certain point you have to start paying for storage, and, again, it is hard to wrap your mind around where everything is when it is out of sight, be it in the cloud or the top of your closet.

The point is, it seems easy to store things digitally, but is it really? Ever tried to make room on your hard drive and opened document after document that you could have thrown out years ago?

There are two things you want to achieve when you are filing digitally. First, you want to be able to access what you are looking for. Second, you want to be able to know what a document is without opening it. Turns out that the key for both of these things is to label (or name) them *consistently.* Whatever your system is—I recommend folders by year or by category and then documents labeled clearly but briefly within them—if you are consistent within your system, you will be able to easily find what you need, and, when it is time to purge, you'll be confident of what you can throw out without laboriously opening each document. If you already had a good paper system, being consistent in labeling across formats will make the transition simpler. As I mentioned in Chapter 6, one of the keys to a good paper system is for every document to have a pathway. If I have determined that I only need to keep receipts for four years and they are properly labeled, deleting those files should be a two-second move, not an excruciating exercise that takes hours.

Cultivating Consistency in Your File Cabinet

If you have paper files, and most people still do, cultivate consistency in your labeling system. Many of my clients have several people in their household, and some prefer to file documents by person. For example, if their child's initials are CAB, we might make a hanging folder called *CAB* and within that *CAB Medical, CAB Academic, CAB Afterschool.* Others prefer to label by category, so they might have a file labeled *Medical* and within that folders for each member of the family.

Give a little thought to the system you want to use. Is it *Tax 2016* or *2016 Tax*, is it *Travel: Italy*, or is *Italy* just a file within *Travel*? This may seem nitpicky, but it will actually help you to conceptualize your system so you can maintain it easily—and more importantly so you can find what you need when you need it.

Keep in mind who will be accessing the files. If it's a household system, for just you or you and your partner, it might be pretty obvious that *Italy* goes into *Travel,* but the bigger the system and the more people who use it, the more detailed you will want to be. For businesses, I always try to include the category name (hanging folder) on the folder label, so that a file on *Marketing* might have within it a folder labeled *Marketing: Print Ads.*

While you are focused on being consistent with your files, think about how you are labeling them. Are you handwriting them? Printing them with a label maker (my favorite)? Printing them off the computer? Use the same color, the same font. You can go all caps or all lowercase, whatever you want; just make a choice and stick with it. It may seem persnickety, but you will be amazed by how much easier the labels are to read when the lettering is consistent.

In the end, consistent labeling of files is a form of politeness. It is not about perfection or showing off but about making life easy for yourself and others. The goal is clarity: you don't have to think too hard or look too hard for a folder, and your eyes don't have to readjust every few seconds.

Consistency as a Decorating Tip

When I was a little girl, my parents took me to many historic buildings in Washington, DC, and Charlottesville, Virginia. What do I remember? Anything about government or history? Nope. I remember that in one building there was a fake door, to create symmetry with the real door. I thought that was great! Three branches of government: boring. Design symmetry: cool.

In fact, as a child I adored things that matched. In high school, my best friend criticized my clothing choices as too matchy-matchy. I still like things to match, although I like to think that I'm not quite as rigid as I was back then. I think matching is restful to the eye; it lends coherence. It's the same with interiors. When you go into someone's home and you can tell there has been thought and care put into the choices, it is soothing.

When we look at the photos in *Real Simple* or *Martha Stewart Living,* often what we are responding to in all these exquisitely "organized" spaces is simply that all the organizing equipment matches. If you are displaying items on exposed shelving, it can be helpful to reduce the visual clutter by having all the boxes match. Sometimes, when clients have glass-front cabinets, I do some swapping so that one color is dominant in the cabinet. By having a color theme it looks more like a collection, less like clutter. Multitudes of framed photographs

continues

continued

can also look cluttery. I say, weed if you can, then swap out the frames so that they all match or coordinate (it doesn't have to be exact, pick a theme such as all silver or all white), then gather them in one spot rather than scattering them around the living area. This way it looks more conscious and planned, less haphazard and random. Then stick to these frames. If you get a great new picture of your kids, swap an old photo out rather than adding another frame to the array.

That said, there's no need to go overboard, especially in spaces that no one will ever see. When I first met with my client Joan, whose photo project was so overwhelming, she showed me the cabinet where her office supplies were stored. They were well organized and labeled. She had used a variety of old stationery and shoeboxes for containers, which worked well. I told her that, yes, we could go buy a bunch of matching white boxes and it would look prettier, but because it was already organized enough, why not save time and money and leave it? Because it was inside a cabinet, she agreed.

Building the Habit

Although I hope that you have made good progress on many, if not all, of the first six habits, cultivating consistency can help you improve any of them. Have you been consistently blocking out time for big projects but still struggling with e-mail? Attack that issue anew by focusing on cultivating consistency.

Like buying less but better, this habit can be challenging to build in a month, but that doesn't mean you shouldn't start. When you begin to cultivate consistency, look at every little thing you do through a different lens: "Why do I empty the dishwasher at different times of day?" "How come some of my towels are folded in thirds and some in half?" As you develop your ability to notice, you will simultaneously be developing the habit of consistency.

As with less but better, I urge you to pick a date and track your progress in your journal. If you're interested in meditation or mindfulness, you should work on applying those principles to your everyday tasks. Be mindful when you shop, when you work at your desk, and as you go about your daily tasks. Bring your whole self to whatever it is you are doing. Ask yourself: "Am I labeling this the same way that I labeled the others?" "Is this the way I decided to keep my grocery list?" "Is buying this dress consistent with the goals I have set for myself? Do I need it? Is it high quality?"

Identifying the Cue

Unlike some of the other habits, this one is hard not because it might not come up very often but because it comes up constantly. You have opportunities to cultivate consistency multiple times a day. Don't feel discouraged because you aren't immediately successful at being consistent with your mail, for example. Stay the course and your efforts to cultivate consistency will pay off eventually, and the rewards will be exponential. You may, without even focusing on them, start to notice improvements in other aspects of your life: the way you wipe down the stovetop or the way you hang up your suit. Just because you are bringing more awareness to those tasks, you are likely to do them more thoughtfully. Although you should try to practice mindfulness and be consistent in all that you do, you may want to pick an area or two to focus on. Your cue should be any time you take an action in any of the areas you are hoping to improve: Doing your ten-minute maintenance? Is that how you filed yesterday? Be mindful.

Some cues you are going to set a day for, like grocery shopping on Monday, and some you are going to tie to an existing habit, like doing your last sweep before you brush your teeth. Still others you are going to have to watch for. Just yesterday, I was walking down Seventy-Second Street, and I thought, "Oh, I'm passing the pet store, I should buy turtle food." "Buy turtle food" was on my to-do list, and seeing the pet store cued me to take care of the errand. However, it's important to differentiate between a cue and a trigger: "Oh, look, there's Old Navy, I bet Sammy needs socks." That's not a cue, that's an impulse purchase. If it isn't on your list, don't do it. Identifying cues and guarding against triggers is the foundational work that will make you succeed at building your habits.

Tracking Your Progress

Don't limit yourself to getting organized. Cultivate consistency in your exercise routine, your habit of reading at bedtime, or putting flax seed on your yogurt in the morning. I truly believe that the ability to cultivate consistency is a muscle, and, when you develop it by applying it to one facet of your life, it will be easier when you try to be consistent in other areas of your life. Practice cultivating consistency on the tiny things that you always mean to do but somehow elude you.

If you go to the gym three days in a week, notice that. Write it down. Give yourself credit. If you go to the gym three days in a week for a month, you are developing a habit. When we work toward cultivating consistency, we pay attention. When we pay attention, we are better able to see the patterns that emerge both in the areas where we are succeeding ("Look at how good this drawer still looks!") and falling short ("Wait, I'm not supposed to have paper towels squished up above the canned goods. What happened?").

Don't be too hard on yourself—remember the goal is to be organized enough. If you just succeed at 50 percent of what I tell you to do in this book, your life is going to be vastly improved.

Your Rewards

Cultivating consistency can help you deepen your commitment to the other habits. For example, if you have made some progress in your inventory control, you may be able to improve your efforts in that area even more by cultivating consistency when you are writing your grocery lists. Maybe you've been much better about limiting your trips to the store, but you are still struggling to stick to one system for your shopping list. Now is a great time to commit to the one you think is the best and spend a few weeks focusing on improving that piece of your habit.

I am busy, I forget things. It is such a relief that I put my keys on the hook by the front door and I returned the flashlight to the utility closet, because if I just had to rely on my memory, I'd be upset frequently. Clients sometimes call me and ask me where something is that we put away together. I don't remember, but I can guess, because I am consistent. Life throws us all kinds of curveballs; it is nice to know that your slippers are in the front hall closet and the chocolate is on the second shelf above the snacks. Because when you want slippers and chocolate, you don't want a hassle.

Consistency means you don't have to remember everything and you can have faith in yourself. And those two things offer quite a bit of relief in a busy world.

We Are Not Perfect

Consistency isn't a habit that you are going to nail in a month. In fact, I wouldn't want you to. Really, it's a practice, a way of approaching the world, and I want you to practice it all the time, forever and ever.

Back when I was an actor I studied the work of Uta Hagen, who was famous for saying, "The body remembers." Her theory was that if you copied the physical manifestation of an emotion, the actual emotion would follow. If you were observant, you would notice how someone in grief doubled over as they were wracked by sobs, and you would imitate that physical response. The great thing about the technique was that even if the actual emotion didn't come, if you were faithful in your rendering of your observations, your audience might never know. In other words: fake it 'til you make it.

So many things I learned to do well are things I originally noticed someone else doing: the way my client Yvette kept her papers, the way the ladies at the laundromat folded everything into perfect rectangular stacks. . . . I'm always observing others' ideas and improving. I wasn't born organized, I've just cultivated that trait in myself until it took root and flourished.

Don't be discouraged if these habits aren't immediately automatic or don't feel organic to you. Just keep faking it, and one day you'll realize that you don't have to fake it anymore—you actually have developed the habit.

It is going to take time. Give yourself time. So what if it takes a year to master staying organized? These habits and methods will serve you for a lifetime. Keep track of your progress and note your successes, not just your slips. It is a process.

Consistency is incredibly rewarding. Soon, you'll instinctively know where everything in your house is and how long it will take to complete tasks. In fact, the rewards are many: less stress, less waste, more serenity, more beauty—to name just a few. The best part about building habits is that, even as it gets easier, the rewards keep coming.

Remember . . .

Cultivating consistency is going to free up your brain for more important things.

Cultivating consistency is key in maintaining inventory (if you are irregular in your laundry/cooking habits, it is hard to keep a constant inventory).

Cultivating consistency eliminates stress. You know where the car keys/passports/immunization records are, because you always put them in the same place.

Conclusion to Part II

"Will I ever be done? Will I ever be organized?" Yes, you will be organized enough, and, no, you will never be done, because life keeps on happening. Just when you have one thing completely under control, something will change and you will have to develop a new system. But that's okay, because you will know how. And your other habits will help you keep sane when the world seems chaotic. If you stay mindful, cultivate consistency, and buy less but better, you will be able to keep your home serene and your possessions under control.

You have the tools and the mind-set: You can use FLOW to remember to be kind to yourself but also to let stuff go. You've rethought the speed at which you move, and you've looked at your space with fresh eyes. You've asked yourself what you are afraid of and who you are. You've confronted your paper and created systems for your home.

You've learned how to create any habit by finding the cue, creating the routine, and keeping your eye on the reward. You've learned about inventory control and structuring your time. You've created boundaries and decided what a neutral state is for your home. Crucially, you're trying to buy less, and when you do it will be better quality. You are practicing your ten-minute maintenance, and you are working on becoming more consistent. I hope you have a renewed relationship with your stuff and to buying, to owning, to discarding.

You don't have to do anything in this book perfectly. If there is one thing that I've learned in life, it's that showing up and being consistent usually trump perfection. Ten-minute maintenance, doing a last sweep before bed, and structuring time on your calendar are all ways of showing up. If we just try day after day, turning our attention to these small matters, our lives will run more smoothly. We will have less stress and more opportunity to enjoy our homes. Perfection is such an airbrushed, stagnant concept. We want our homes to be dynamic, vital places, but at the same time we don't want them to be chaotic. My hope is that the concepts and the habits in this book will help you to achieve that balance: to be organized enough.

Forget perfection: it's a false god. What we want is joy, serenity, and to know where we put the car keys—and those things, my friends, are within your grasp.

RESOURCES

Baumeister, Roy F., and John Tierney. *Willpower: Rediscovering the Greatest Human Strength.* New York: Penguin, 2012.

Currey, Mason. *Daily Rituals.* London: Picador, 2014.

Duhigg, Charles. *The Power of Habit.* New York: Random House, 2012.

Huffington, Arianna. *Thrive.* New York: Harmony, 2014.

Lanier, Jaron. *You Are Not a Gadget.* New York: Vintage Books, 2011.

Lazarovic, Sarah. *A Bunch of Pretty Things I Did Not Buy.* New York: Penguin, 2014.

Levine, Judith. *Not Buying It: My Year Without Shopping.* New York: Free Press, 2006.

Pollan, Michael. *In Defense of Food.* New York: Penguin Press, 2008.

Rubin, Gretchen. *The Happiness Project.* New York: Harper, 2009.

Turkle, Sherry. *Reclaiming Conversation.* New York: Penguin Press, 2015.

Yarrow, Kit. *Decoding the New Consumer Mind.* San Francisco: Jossey-Bass, 2014.

ACKNOWLEDGMENTS

No woman is an island, and I have had so much help from so many people in the process of writing this book.

Katie Kretschmer: How fortunate that a hyphen-abusing writer like me should happen to have an editor extraordinaire for a best friend. Thank you for reading this book almost as often as I did—and every other word I have written since graduate school. If I'd only thought to ask you to edit my work in middle school, I would have done much better.

Ellen Scordato, Maria Ribas and all of the team at Stonesong: You held me to a high standard and then you pushed me up to it. Thank you.

Renee Sedliar and everyone at Da Capo: Thank you for all of your patience and wisdom guiding me through this process, especially Katie Malm McHugh, who spent so many hours helping to refine the manuscript.

Sarah Rivera: Thank you for your vision and your nudging; it was just what I needed.

Valerie Markwood: You sent me to the New York Writer's Workshop, and that got the ball rolling. Thank you.

Lisa Sharkey Gleicher: The first day I worked for you in 2000, you asked, "Are you writing a book?" And I thought, There are books about this?

Pamela Miles: You made me see my work not as something merely secretarial or janitorial, but as something healing.

Romaine Orthwein, Judith Vogel, Bettijane Eisenpreis: Thank you for being there, always.

The Saturday Night Crew: Thank you for keeping me sane and keeping it real.

Finally, to my extremely neat and incredibly patient husband, Gary Bernstein, and our three glorious and unique children, Henry, Simone, and Bobby. Like the song says, "Everything I do, I do for you."

INDEX

ABOUT THE AUTHOR

Amanda Sullivan is a Professional Organizer, and founder of *The Perfect Daughter: Chaos Control*. Amanda has been creating order out of chaos since the seventh grade, when she tackled lockers and desks before dreaded inspections. After college, she segued from working for a temp agency to organizing the temp agency. In 1999, she went into the organizing business full time, and since then she has since helped hundreds of clients, from hoarders to celebrities. Amanda has appeared on *Good Morning America* and *Living it Up with Ali and Jack* with Jack Ford and Ali Wentworth Stephanopoulos. Her advice has appeared in national print magazines such as *Woman's Day* and *Fit Pregnancy*, as well as on popular Web sites such as *Next Avenue* and *About.com*.

Amanda lives in Manhattan with her husband, her three children, nineteen feet of bookshelves, and plenty of imperfection. When she isn't organizing her clients or her kids she likes to throw overly elaborate parties or, if her husband's not up for that, send her kids out so she can read *The New York Times* in peace. She's a Sagittarius, not a Virgo, which is why she keeps her eye on the goal and doesn't get caught up in the minutiae.

theperfectdaughter.com